BUSTIN' THROUGH THE ROOF

Ordinary Folks, Extraordinary Faith

MICHAEL D. KURTZ, D MIN, LMFT

Also, by Michael D. Kurtz
Everyday Life in the Times of the Judges, Included in Abingdon's Bible Teacher Kit
Approaching the New Millennium: Biblical End-Time Images
Lessons From a Christmas Tree Farm: A Devotional and Study Guide Resource
Crossings: Memoirs of a Mountain Medical Doctor
Michael's Musings: A Pastor Blogs on Life
Mentoring Pew Sitters into Servant Leaders
Overcoming Odds and Obstacles: The Story of a State Championship Team

BUSTIN' THROUGH THE ROOF

ORDINARY FOLKS, EXTRAORDINARY FAITH

iUniverse books may be ordered through booksellers or by contacting:

iUniverse
1663 Liberty Drive
Bloomington, IN 47403
www.iuniverse.com
844-349-9409

Because of the dynamic nature of the Internet, any web addresses or links contained in this book may have changed since publication and may no longer be valid. The views expressed in this work are solely those of the author and do not necessarily reflect the views of the publisher, and the publisher hereby disclaims any responsibility for them.

Any people depicted in stock imagery provided by Getty Images are models, and such images are being used for illustrative purposes only. Certain stock imagery © Getty Images.

ISBN: 978-1-6632-5759-8 (sc)
ISBN: 978-1-6632-5774-1 (e)

Library of Congress Control Number: 2024926108

Print information available on the last page.

iUniverse rev. date: 12/17/2024

THIS BOOK IS DEDICATED TO THE GLORY OF GOD WHO HAS GRACIOUSLY PLACED THE ORDINARY AND BEAUTIFULLY BROKEN SAINTS IN OUR LIVES WHO HAVE LIFTED US TO JESUS.

Mark 2:1-5 (CEB):

"After a few days, Jesus went back to Capernaum, and people heard that he was at home. So many gathered that there was no longer space, not even near the door. Jesus was speaking the word to them. Some people arrived, and four of them were bringing to him a man who was paralyzed. They couldn't carry him through the crowd, so they tore off part of the roof above where Jesus was. When they had made an opening, they lowered the mat on which the paralyzed man was lying. When Jesus saw their faith, he said to the paralytic, 'Child, your sins are forgiven!'"

Table of Contents

1   Lillie – Forgiveness 1

2   Paul – Commitment 7

3   Lillie Mae – Missions 11

4   Aunt Jean – Aging Gracefully...15

5   Otis – Hunger for the Word 19

6   Dad – Pioneer and Peace Advocate 23

7   Mom – Lessons and Blessings...27

8   Gray – Heaven's Acolyte 31

9   Claude – Once Blind but Now I See 35

10 Emma - Genuine Humility 41

11 Rudy – A Wise Counselor 45

12 Norman – A Mentor 49

13 Jim – Singing the Song Placed Within 53

14 Paul and Rachel – Teaching the Word 59

15 John and Joan – Grace and Generosity 65

16 Granddaddy – Steady and Reliable 69

17 My Karen – Noble Character 73

18 Anna and Joshua – And a Child Shall Lead Them 79

19 Non-Anxious Supportive Presence 85

20 Grandpa and Grandma – Discipleship and Simplicity..............................89

21 Dori – Tender-Hearted and Tough-Skinned 95

22 Sam and Linda – A Place of Sanctuary 101

23 Reggie – A Merry Heart...105

24 Hagey – A Surrogate Grandparent 107

25 Betty Jo – A Willing Spirit, A Servant's Heart, An Open Mind 111

26 Keith – Good Chemistry 115

SUGGESTED USES:

-Individual Devotional

Resource

-A Month of Reflections

-Twenty-six group sessions

(Two Calendar Quarters)

FORWARD

"We are called to be the church: to celebrate God's presence, to love and serve others, to seek justice and resist evil, to proclaim Jesus, crucified and risen, our judge and our hope. In life, in death, in life beyond death, God is with us. We are not alone. Thanks be to God. Amen." (p. 883 UMH, A Statement of Faith of the United Church of Canada).

For almost seven decades, I have been challenged, nurtured, and loved in and by the broken and beloved Body of Christ, the Church. Baptized and confirmed into a faith that would stretch me beyond my wildest imagination, I still believe more strongly than ever in the power of the Church Community to make disciples of Jesus Christ for the transformation of the world.

Ordinary, flawed saints along the journey have shown me the face of Christ. Like the four faithful friends who broke through a thatched roof to lift their friend to Jesus, the Church Community has embodied gritty tenacity, grace, messiness and a whole lot of faithfulness as they have simply loved people like me enough to usher us into His presence, breaking barriers along the way.

These stories are only representative of the vast myriads of consistent and beautiful saints who have inspired Michael and me over the decades of parish ministry. Though imperfect, these fellow sojourners, many who are now part of the heavenly Communion of Saints, intentionally loved people into the nearer Presence of Christ. They remind us poignantly of why Jesus believed in his Bride, and why that holy call must ever guide the Church forward, busting through the obstacles that might separate and hinder us. Whether from a Hospice bed, a hospital ICU, a prison, or a Sunday school class, these faithful on the following pages – and so many like them – have lifted us closer to the Master. For that we are eternally grateful. Thank you for being the church.

Karen C. Kurtz

2024

INTRODUCTION

We all have people in our lives along the journey who have had a positive and permanent influence upon us. Their influence left an indelible impact. What a gift! Life is not intended to be navigated alone. We need others. Others need us. And we need one another. Gerhard E. Frost expresses this human interdependence in his poem titled:

HEZEKIAH 6:14

"'The reason mountain climbers are tied together is to keep the sane ones from going home.' I don't know who said it, or when, or where, but I've chuckled over it, thought about it, and quoted it, too.

With a mountain of mercy behind me and a mountain of mission ahead, I need you, my sister, my brother, I need to be tied to you, and you need me, too.

We need each other…to keep from bolting, fleeing in panic, and returning to the 'sanity' of unbelief. Wise words, whoever said them; I've placed them in my 'bible'; they are my Hezekiah 6:14."

In the Gospel of Mark, chapter 2, we locate a powerful story which poignantly pictures four compassionate persons, taking a crippled man, a man in need, to Jesus. These friends see a need, and they lovingly respond. They display deep concern for this paralytic, going out of their way, probably changing their plans for the day, so that this man may find help. They are determined and persistent, meeting and overcoming roadblocks, as they carry the cripple to Christ. Yet, when they are met with these roadblocks and detours, being unable to get the man through the crowd which has gathered around Jesus, they creatively and determinedly go to plan B. They go bustin' through the roof! Dr. Luke informs us, "When they could not find a way to get the man to Jesus because of the crowd, they went up on the roof and lowered him on his mat through the tiles into the middle of the crowd, right in front of Jesus."

Wow! Can you see it? These men, to get their crippled friend to Jesus, stop at nothing! They realize what their friend needs, which only Jesus can provide. So, whatever it takes! If the crowd is so thick that they can't get to Jesus through the door, or even through a window, then they'll go up on the roof! Remove some roof tiles. Lower the man right in front of Jesus. The very best for their needy friend. Front row seats! No sitting in the waiting area! Delivered directly to the Great Physician's examination room. Eyeball to eyeball with the Healer himself! What a gift! What a sacred treasure, to experience someone bringing you closer to Jesus! Very often it is in hindsight when we recognize and realize a relationship encounter which has assisted in our positive faith formation.

In this book, I invite and encourage you, the reader, to consider, remember, and give thanks for the influencers, those who have helped in the forming of your faith. Who are the people in your pilgrimage on this ball of clay, who have assisted in pointing you to Jesus along the way? Recall them. Perhaps call them (or a text or note) if they are still this side of the Jordan. And, above all, give gratitude to God for these influential individuals in your life. Perhaps they "busted through roof tiles" for you. Maybe it was something considered less dramatic than the roof scene. Yet let us never forget, the so-called mundane, small words and actions can have a powerful and permanent impact upon us. As I share a representative portion of people who God has placed, and used, in my life to help show Jesus to me, may you also remember those tainted – broken but beautiful - saints in your life and be grateful.

CHAPTER ONE

LILLIE

Forgiveness

*Refusing to forgive, and holding on to bitterness, is like drinking
poison and waiting for the other person to die. -Unknown*

Lillie was a simple, quiet and humble lady. She was a farmer who loved to plant, cultivate and harvest crops on the land. She raised crops and she and her husband Ed, reared five sons. Lillie faithfully tended to the farm. And she lovingly raised her boys.

One sunny spring day an unthinkable, tragic event occurred that would forever change Lillie's life. Her youngest son, a teenager, was riding a motorcycle on a local highway, not two miles from their home. He was hit by another vehicle in a hit-and-run encounter. This horrible, senseless wreck left Lillie's son dead, as well as the friend riding with him.

With prompt and persistent law enforcement detective efforts the hit-and-run driver was identified, apprehended and placed in the local jail. Lillie and Ed were, understandably, crushed by the loss of their son. Although they were grateful the perpetrator was found and being brought to some measure of justice, no amount of justice could bring back their son.

I was blessed to serve as Lillie and Ed's pastor for several years. I was their pastor when this parental nightmare occurred. As I reflect upon Lillie's Jesus-following Walk, I am reminded of her quiet and reserved witness. Frequently serving behind the scenes. Rarely speaking out. Never seeking the limelight. She was one of those steady, reliable, willing helpers, behind the scenes. Her mode of operation reminded me of a famous quote which goes something like this: "Preach the gospel. If necessary, use words." That was Lillie. Laconic. Quiet servant. A life which evidenced the Light of Christ.

In this spirit and style of walking the walk, not so much talking the talk – an approach which seems sorely lacking in Christian circles – Lillie, as concerns her son's tragic death, provided me, and our entire congregation a sermon which shall never be forgotten! After Lillie learned that the hit-and-run driver who had killed her son, along with a second victim, was incarcerated at the local jail, she chose to do something which most persons would be incapable of doing, or surely refuse to do.

The Sunday morning after her son was killed, which occurred on the prior Monday afternoon, Lillie approached Ed and requested that he drive her downtown to the local jail, where the prisoner was incarcerated. Ed agreed and they went to the jailhouse. Lillie requested, and was granted, permission to visit (through a plexiglass partition) with the offender who had killed her son and then fled the scene.

As witnessed and relayed by the jailer, Lillie looked the inmate in his eyes and stated, "You killed my son, and you have crushed my heart. But I am a Christian and I am taught by Jesus to forgive you. I do forgive you. But I surely hope you make things right with the Lord!"

With those words Lillie turned around; walked out of the detention center; got into the car where Ed was waiting, and they headed to Sunday morning worship at our church! What an amazing, unforgettable (even unimaginable) sermon on forgiveness!

Through Lillie's seemingly humanly impossible, yet God-guided, act of mercy, all of us in our church family were amazed, inspired, and we were pointed to the amazing grace and mercy of Jesus. In Matthew's gospel, the 6th chapter, for example, Jesus instructs: "If you forgive others their sins, your heavenly Father will also forgive you. But if you don't forgive others, neither will your father forgive your sins" (Matthew 6:14,15).

Interestingly, these words of Jesus appear immediately following The Lord's Prayer, in which our Savior provides us a model, all-encompassing, cover-it-all, prayer. And of all the topics Jesus covers in The Lord's Prayer – from "hallowed" be God's name, to requesting daily food to eat, to forgiving others, to overcoming evil – Jesus returns, right after teaching the prayer, to the subject of forgiveness. How central to life and living is forgiveness!

How difficult it is to offer forgiveness; yet, how essential it is to forgive so that we may obediently follow Christ, leading us to a path of liberty and tranquility. Lillie refused to give in to a life of hate and resentment (albeit much more quickly doing so than I could ever imagine myself doing in that context). Those of us who knew Lillie, who watched her everyday life, witnessed how she based her life upon the love, grace and forgiveness of God. Through her gentleness and humility, that which was of God was experienced and evidenced in Lillie's persona.

GENTLENESS and HUMILITY CONNECTED WITH FORGIVENESS

Gentleness and humility are prerequisites for practicing genuine forgiveness. A spirit of gentleness enables the mercy path (loving kindness) to be followed. Humility provides the much-needed realization that we stand continually in need of God's grace and forgiveness. It is fascinating, and instructive, that Jesus, in scripture, uses only two words (characteristics) with which to self-describe: gentle and humble! In Matthew 11:28,29, we are told: "Come to me, all you who are struggling hard and carrying heavy loads, and I will give you rest. Put on my yoke and learn from me. I'm gentle and humble. And you will find rest for yourselves." Through Christ's gentleness and humility, we receive acceptance and forgiveness. And through "putting on Christ's yoke," we take on the gentle and humble persona, and we are enabled and empowered to extend forgiveness to ourselves and to others.

RECOGNIZING OUR NEED FOR FORGIVENESS

There are at least three parts and practices to the forgiveness factor. The first step in forgiveness is that we must recognize our need for forgiveness. This is the primary and continual status for each and all of us. As we realize and confess our sinfulness, our shortcomings, we then approach God, and others with humility and with gratitude.

This forgiveness thing is for everyone, because "all have fallen short of the glory of God." In authentic confession we begin with our personal recognition of our own sin, not projecting (pointing accusingly at another) upon another. We begin with the proverbial "plank" in our own eye, not the "splinter" in the eye of another. We herein own, acknowledge, and repent of our sin and brokenness before holy, righteous God. Thereby we go to The Source of ultimate and complete forgiveness. At the feet of Jesus, The Source of forgiveness, we discover the "re-source" through which we forgive self and extend forgiveness to others. In the words of a Christian hymn, "It's me, it's me, O Lord, standing in the need of prayer. Not my brother. Not my sister. But it's me, O Lord. Standing in the need of prayer."

WE FORGIVE OURSELVES

As we locate, and assimilate, God's gracious grace we are opening and receiving a precious and healing gift. We acknowledge the Gift-Giver. We open and accept the gift. We are cleansed, liberated, and reconciled with our Creator.

To not accept this gift by refusing to forgive oneself is preposterous and audacious. Not accepting God's gift of grace is unbelief. It is a lack of trust in Divinity. Sometimes we seem to have a longer memory than God, so we rationalize. The written Word proclaims, "If we confess our sins, God is faithful and just and will forgive us all our unrighteousness" (I John 1:9). If God forgives us, which God promises He does upon our confession, then who are we to not forgive ourselves?!

Yet, our human condition is often that while God forgives and forgets our sin, as we confess, we, in tragic and stark contrast, cling to our guilt and sin, permitting it to make of us slaves. Therefore, we carry all this guilt-garbage around with us. A heavy, smelly burden! Our sins piling up like debts, like smelly trash. We can never pay this debt. We can never get rid of our own garbage. And God offers: "I release you from that debt! I will take all that garbage! I make for you a trade – My grace for your garbage – which will free you from guilt so that you may share this liberty with others.

Still, we frequently stubbornly cling to our garbage. The reality is we cannot enter through the kingdom of heaven's narrow door with our bulging garbage bags. Because the kingdom of heaven is for repentant sinners only. When we are truly repentant, we let go and with open, empty hands we receive what can only be given by God, no longer a slave to the burdensome garbage of sin.

The Jesus-following forgiveness path is not only recognition and confession and repentance of our sin. It is also accepting and receiving that forgiveness of God so that we may forgive ourselves, so that we do not carry all that guilt and garbage around, stinking up our lives and the lives of others.

On this forgiveness path we believe and receive the forgiveness of God. We forgive ourselves because God, in Christ, has forgiven us.

WE FORGIVE OTHERS

There is another portion on this forgiveness path. We pass forgiveness on. We show forgiveness and mercy to others. "Forgive us our trespasses as we forgive those who trespass against us." Sometimes we go around grabbing others by the neck, not letting them go for a $20 debt, while we have been forgiven a twenty- million-dollar debt from Divinity! (See Mathew 18:21-35, The Parable of the Unforgiving Servant).

As we really recognize what God has done for us, how much mercy we have received in our confession, there results genuine humility and great gratitude unto God. So much gratitude, in fact, overflowing gratitude, to the point that we are willing to extend undeserved mercy to others!

If we fail to extend this mercy; if we withhold forgiveness from others, we are wounding ourselves. Someone has profoundly put it, "Bitterness is like drinking poison and waiting for the other person to die."

Forgiveness is not an easy thing. It is hard work. Especially difficult when we have been badly, unjustly wronged. Yet it will wither our souls and potentially kill us spiritually and emotionally, and possibly physically, if we do not let go of our bitterness and resentment and forgive the other. Just ask Lillie.

SCRIPTURE READINGS: Isaiah 55:7; Psalm 32:5; Luke 6:37; Ephesians 4:31-32; Colossians 3:1-3; James 5:16

QUESTIONS FOR REFLECTION AND DISCUSSION:
1. How do you respond to Lillie's practice of forgiveness?
2. In what ways might gentleness and humility be associated with forgiveness?
3. What thoughts and feelings do you experience as you hear the words of scripture, "For all have sinned and fallen short of the glory of God?"
4. Our human condition reminds us that we find it hard to forgive ourselves. Reflect upon and discuss this human status.
5. Before we can truly forgive another person, we must receive God's forgiveness and forgive ourselves. Do you agree with this two-part statement? Why or why not?

PRAYER:

Gracious God, thank you for your amazing grace! May we be completely honest with you. You alone, O God, are holy and righteous. We are unrighteous and broken. We have done what we should not have done. We have not done what we should have done. In your mercy, hear our prayer and forgive. As we confess and receive your unmerited and undeserved forgiveness may we extend forgiveness to others. For the cause of Christ, we pray. Amen.

CHAPTER TWO

PAUL

Commitment

"If nothing lasts forever, then what's forever for?" - Lyrics
to song, "What's Forever For," Rafe Van Hoy

When I think of marital faithfulness and commitment, the honoring of marriage vows, my mind often goes to Paul. Paul was a dedicated husband. A faithful spouse. In our United Methodist Service of Christian Marriage, the Declaration of Intention, asks of both partners to be married:

"Will you have the 'other' to be your 'spouse', to live together in holy marriage? Will you love them, comfort them, honor and keep them, in sickness and in health, and forsaking all others, be faithful to them as long as you both shall live?"

Both persons have the opportunity and obligation to respond with, "I will."

"Will you love them, comfort them, honor and keep them, in sickness and in health?" In this spirit of marital compassion and covenant, I witnessed Paul's tender care for his bride (Bea) of over sixty years. Bea suffered from severe dementia. Paul kept Bea at their home for as long as he possibly could. But the time came when he could no longer look after her many needs. He needed help. So, with a grieved heart, Paul placed Bea in a nursing home.

A MARITAL COVENANT DISPLAYED

Every day, without fail, Paul would go to Bea's room at the nursing home, lovingly and patiently feeding her meals to her, one slow spoonful at a time. Then, following lunch, he would brush her long silver hair and while doing so he would repeat to her over and over, "Bea, I love you. I will always love you!" As their pastor, I counted it a holy privilege to, on occasion, be seated in the same room experiencing this intimate and beautiful, yet painful, relational commitment scene.

Taking the path of total and radical commitment to another, given taxing circumstances, was difficult, at times overwhelming. Yet, Paul had committed over sixty years ago to a permanent, lifetime marital covenant with Bea. And he was a man of his word. Besides, he would say to me, when I inquired of his sacrifice, "She would do the very same for me."

After Bea died Paul stated, "Those were long, hard years of care for Bea, but I wouldn't do it any other way. It may sound strange to hear, but Bea blessed me during the nursing home days in ways I can't understand or explain. I have no regrets."

The way of covenant-commitment-and-care. A life and a lifestyle that is trustworthy and faithful. Those of us who watched Paul's loving nurture of Bea were encouraged, challenged and inspired.

DIVINE COVENANT ENABLES, EMPOWERS HUMAN COMMITMENT

Yet Paul would be one to say that the love and commitment he manifested with Bea came from a Source beyond him. The kind of unconditional love evidenced between Paul and Bea was created, enabled and empowered by and through God. God is love. God gives to us a love so that we may love one another. This agape love is offered to us by a covenant God. A God who longs to be in a love relationship with each of us, God's children!

It is a faithful God in whom we trust. It is a compassionate, merciful God through whom we love. We may always rely upon God's steadfast concern and care for us. It is through the unfailing faithfulness of God by which we are secure and nurtured so that we may extend commitment and care to others.

In the words of a classic Christian hymn:

"Great is thy faithfulness, O God my Father; there is no shadow of turning with thee; thou changest not, thy compassions, they fail not; as thou hast been, thou forever wilt be. (Chorus): Great is thy faithfulness! Great is thy faithfulness! Morning by morning new mercies I see; all I have needed thy hand has provided; great is thy faithfulness, Lord, unto me" (United Methodist Hymnal, page 140)!

GOD'S CONDITIONAL, ETERNAL LOVE DESCRIBED

This agape, faithful love is impossible for us to practice and model on our own. It can only be genuinely generated and given to one another in the human family through God working in, and imputing to, us God's grace and mercy. The perfect, unconditional love of God is too high a bar for us to reach on our own, by ourselves. Saint Paul, in the thirteenth chapter of First Corinthians, provides a description of this divine love, using sixteen adjectives which unpack this heavenly love in a down-to-earth picture. The word used by

Paul for love in First Corinthians, chapter thirteen, is "agape," - God's divine, amazing, unconditional love and compassion.

Consider and ponder the description of God's love for us, which then enables and empowers our human love for one another: "Love is patient, love is kind, it isn't jealous, it doesn't brag, it isn't arrogant, it isn't rude, it doesn't seek its own advantage, it isn't irritable, it doesn't keep a record of complaints, it isn't happy with injustice, but it is happy with the truth. Love puts up with all things, trusts in all things, hopes for all things, endures all things. Love never fails" (First Corinthians 13:4-8a).

Wow! Talk about radical love! A totally unconditional love and acceptance of another! This First Corinthians' unpacking of Agape love should humble even the most loving human being on their very best day of loving!

A COVENANT COMMITMENT CONTINUES

Paul was committed to Bea. He loved her to the best of his ability. Yet, Paul would speak of his impatience and irritability at times with his now totally dependent bride. Their relationship was vastly different. Some days were so long and difficult. Many times, Paul did not know if Bea even knew who he was. Yet, there were breakthrough moments, once in a great while, when the true and remembered personality of Bea showed through. There were some rare and treasured moments when Bea looked deeply into Paul's eyes, seemingly with mutual recognition, and there was a deep respect and connection transfer, which they had shared so many times before, for so many years in their journey together as husband and wife! In sickness and in health, in good times and in tough times, through divine faithfulness, human commitment persevered.

May we seek to more deeply experience, and express, God's great and gracious covenant love through good times and in tough times as we are enabled and empowered by divine commitment. Let us seek to strengthen God's Kingdom on earth as in heaven, through abiding love and enduring commitment.

SCRIPTURE REFERENCES: Genesis 2:24; Deuteronomy 7:9; Psalm 103:17-18; Isaiah 54:10; Ephesians 4:1-3; Hebrews 9:15.

QUESTIONS FOR REFLECTION AND DISCUSSION:
1. In the Christian marriage "Declaration of Intention," what is declared? Why?
2. How might you be encouraged and/or challenged by the relationship between Bea and Paul?
3. Do you affirm God's commitment to us enables our commitment to one another? If so, how so?
4. Recount the sixteen characteristics of God's agape love (First Corinthians, chapter 13). Select one or two characteristics that need attention in your life.
5. Define covenant. How does "covenant" differ from "contract"?

PRAYER:

Covenant, Faithful God,

You are love, and it is through your love that we are even able to love one another. Forgive us for our broken relationships. We are so quick to give up on ourselves, and on others when the going gets tough. In our consumer culture we are accustomed to discarding the old, the used and broken. We even discard relationships, maintaining its "My way, or the highway!" Lord, thank you for your patient kindness and constant acceptance of us, your wayward children. Help us live in covenant relationships, grounded in and motivated by your continual and undeserved commitment to us! For Christ's cause, we pray. Amen.

CHAPTER THREE

LILLIE MAE

Missional Outreach

"Pray globally, Act locally." – Patrick Geddes

Every Tuesday morning, at ten o'clock, about a dozen ladies would gather in the old country farmhouse kitchen where Lillie Mae lived. For nearly thirty years they met for Bible study, fellowship, followed by a covered dish luncheon. Each week they lifted an offering to help support missionaries throughout the world. On occasion, when on furlough, some of the missionaries supported by this ladies' Bible study, would visit in the farmhouse with this small group.

Lillie Mae had a passion and a vision for outreach and missions. She prayed for and supported various peoples and places around the world. Ironically, Lillie Mae did not drive and for the first seventy-six years of her life she had never been out of the United States, and rarely out of North Carolina. Yet, despite living a "limited lifestyle," as many might say, Lillie Mae touched the entire world through prayer and financial resources. Through a small group of ladies gathered regularly in a rural farmhouse kitchen, lives around the globe were encouraged and positively impacted, both physically and spiritually. Through their financial offerings, food, both physical and spiritual, was provided for the hungry. Years later, after Lillie Mae had died, and the ladies' Bible study had disbanded, a journal with a ledger kept by the ladies was located. The ledger carefully detailed and recorded each week's offering amount, coins and dollar bills given consistently by these simple, country women. Over the thirty years of meeting, the journal showed the group had raised more than $31,000.00 donated to missions for the cause of Christ!

AN ADVOCATE FOR MISSION OUTREACH

Lillie Mae faithfully supported our church and local community ministries. Yet, Lillie Mae shared her worldwide mission vision, not only with the ladies' small group meeting in her home. She also enabled and inspired our congregation to plant and grow a vision for national and international missions in Jesus' name. Whenever our church convened a council meeting, if Lillie Mae was in attendance, she would always advocate for mission outreach. And she was not shy about it! She expressed the missional needs, did her research and presented the research results. Her assertive and diplomatic style won over most congregants, including the church leadership team. As a result, the church to which Lillie Mae belonged, and where I was blessed to pastor for six years, allotted no less than ten percent (a tithe) of their annual budget to national and international missions each year. This helped us keep an outward focus and assisted in keeping us more attentive to how God is working in the entire world, not only in our small corner of the universe.

WHEN LITTLE BECOMES MUCH

God can and will use one person to make a big difference. If, by faith in God, we bring what we have and offer it to be employed in the Kingdom, significant things can happen. Lillie Mae, I believe, is proof of this principle. In an old hymn of the Christian faith this multiplication mystery is asserted, as the lyrics affirm, "Little is much when God is in it." Lillie Mae had little formal education. She never obtained a driver's license. She rarely got out of her rural farm home, unless someone arrived at her door to drive her places she could not reach on her own. She did not possess a lot, materially speaking. Yet, she offered what limited resources she had, and through this offering and giving lives were impacted, literally around the world!

A simple woman, with limited material resources, yet with a Spirit-inspired vision and passion, showed many of us the path to authentic joy through Kingdom outreach. So it was, with great anticipation and excitement, that our church family collected a special mission offering for a special lady. During her seventy-seventh year of life, we sent Lillie Mae on a two-week mission trip to Costa Rica! You would have thought we had given her the world. Which, of course, we had. Because now she was literally going to see and touch firsthand a portion of the world she had, for years, touched through prayer! For Lillie Mae, who had never stepped foot on international soil; yet, who had helped ensure support for many missionaries in many countries over the years, was now the recipient of one of her life-long dreams – to go to another land, one she had supported from her farmhouse kitchen!

Rarely have I observed someone so motivated and so appreciative as Lillie Mae, as we took her to the airport. There were tears streaming down her cheeks as we bid her farewell for her two-week mission experience. Tears of joy! Upon her return from Costa Rica, she presented a testimony to our congregation. She gave an overview of the mission team's work and missional activity. She thanked the congregation for this "trip of a lifetime," and then she ended her remarks by stating, "Thank you, my church family, for the gift of this mission trip opportunity. Because of this experience I will never be the same!"

SHARING THE GOOD NEWS WITH OTHERS

One of Lillie Mae's signature scriptures echoes in my mind as I reflect upon her life and as I recall her passion for missions: "You will receive power when the Holy Spirit has come upon you, and you will be my witnesses in Jerusalem, in all Judea and Samaria, and to the end of the earth" -Jesus (Acts 1:8).

For those of us who knew Lillie Mae, she inspired us to reach out to others with the Good News of Jesus Christ. This Good News is too good to keep to ourselves. We are called to share with others – locally, nationally and internationally – for the sake of God's Kingdom.

In the words of a Christian hymn: "Help me in all the work I do; To ever be sincere and true. And know that all I'd do for You, must needs be done for others. Others, Lord, yes, others, let this my motto be. Help me to live for others, that I may live like Thee" (The Cokesbury Worship Hymnal; Abingdon Press, page 177. C D Meigs; Elizabeth Shields).

Like Lillie Mae, may we touch the world through prayer. Like Lillie Mae, may we offer what little we may have to help make the world a better place for the cause of the Kingdom. In Jesus' name may we reach out to others.

SCRIPTURE REFERENCES: Isaiah 57:7; Jeremiah 1:7; Matthew 24:11-14; Matthew 25:35-40; Matthew 28:19-20; Acts 20:24.

QUESTIONS FOR REFLECTION AND DISCUSSION:
1. What lessons might we take from Lillie Mae's ladies' farmhouse prayer group?
2. Are there examples that come to mind when thinking of the lyrics, "Little is much when God is in it"?
3. How do you respond to the statement, "Pray globally and act locally"?
4. Through the internet and social media our world is more electronically connected than ever. Yet, ironically, with many wonderful relational tools in our hands, we find ourselves isolated and estranged. What actions might we take to be better connected to people both near and far?
5. As a legal expert once asked Jesus, "And who is my neighbor?", so too we are faced with that very same question, especially as Jesus followers. How do you define "neighbor"? (Perhaps give Luke 10:25-37 a look to be informed of Jesus' response to this important question).

PRAYER:

God, Creator of all People, Everywhere,

Give us a heart for the entire world which you have made. Forgive our narrow-mindedness and ethnocentric way of thinking and living. May we pray for, reach out to, and care about people near and far. O Loving Lord, every human being is fashioned in Your sacred image. Help us to view others with the eyes of Christ and enable us to love others with the heart of Jesus. In so doing, may your will be done on earth as it is in heaven. For the cause and mission of Christ, we pray. Amen.

CHAPTER FOUR

AUNT JEAN

Aging Graciously and Gracefully

"Those who love deeply never grow old; they may die of
old age, but they die young." – Benjamin Franklin

We all called her "Aunt Jean" although she was technically my wife's great aunt. Jean lived to one hundred and eleven years of age! She not only lived a life large in quantity, but also a life of great quality. She loved to read, enjoyed walking, socializing with friends in her small southern mountain town, served her church, and taught high school English for more than forty years.

A HEALTHY SENSE OF HUMOR

One of Aunt Jean's "school rules" was that no boy could ever wear a cap in her classroom. Never ever! She strictly enforced this rule. She was from the old school, which meant wearing a cap in the classroom was a sign of disrespect. Guys should remove their caps upon entering the classroom, or any room.

After she retired from teaching some of us in the family concocted a plan to tease Jean. We had caps custom made with "Aunt Jean Caps" embroidered across the front of each hat. One summer when several of us were visiting Jean for her 106th birthday we all wore these customized caps in Jean's home. As we walked into her house and paraded right in front of her in her living room, at first, she seemed shocked. Then a big smile broke out on her face. There was a sparkle in her eyes as she said, "You boys are crazy! But I love each one of you!" Jean possessed a wonderful and contagious sense of humor.

Jean, even at the ripe age of one-hundred-and-six, could laugh at herself. She did not take herself too seriously. On one occasion I asked Aunt Jean what the secret was to her longevity. Without pausing, she responded while laughing, "I never had a man to bring me down!" Jean had never been married. She was quite independent and content and happy with the single life. Her life was rich and fulfilling with extended family, teaching, community relationships and a commitment to Christ. What a gift to age gracefully and graciously! How wonderful it is, increasing in years while at the same time growing in kindness and grace toward others. Avoiding rigidity. Staying open minded and flexible. Sharing your life and experience, while also learning from others. Giving and taking. Always something to learn from every person.

CONTINUALLY LEARNING; REFUSING TO CONGEAL

Folks like Aunt Jean are enjoyable to be around and to have around. It is good to be in their presence because they have a posture of openness – to life and to others. They are people who continue to learn and grow. They are living testimonies to an old 4-H motto, which stated, "If you're green, you're growing. If you're ripe, you're rotting." As author Gail Godwin puts it, "There are two kinds of people. One kind, you can tell just by looking at them at what point they congealed into their final selves. It might be a nice enough self, but you know you can expect no more surprises from it. Whereas the other kind keeps moving, changing. They are fluid. They keep moving forward and making new trysts with life, and the motion of it keeps them young. In my opinion, they are the only people who are still alive. You must be constantly on your guard, against congealing" (Viking Press, 1984; p4).

Jean did not congeal. Until the final year of her life, at age one-hundred-and-eleven, she continued to maintain an open posture to living. She had opinions which she was not shy to share that is for sure. Yet, she always listened to the other and to other opinions. She was willing to talk about politics, social issues and religion while continually remembering her position was not the only position. For certain, she had her deeply held convictions and firmly formed opinions. Yet, given her age and stage of life it was truly amazing to observe her open-mindedness! She had seen so many changes during her lifetime. For instance, there were no motorized vehicles in her town when she was a young girl. This reality recalls Toffler's "Future Shock," which speaks to the enormity of change and cultural transformations within the span of even a few decades. Aunt Jean had seen and lived through many of these radical changes, yet she somehow kept a learning posture and a flexible spirit.

AGING GRACEFULLY AND GRACIOUSLY

Aunt Jean evidenced aging gracefully and graciously. She exemplified maintaining an open posture to life throughout many and varied cultural changes. Jean displayed the healthy and humble personality trait of not taking herself too seriously. She regularly shared a sense of humor and could easily laugh at herself. She kept a positive disposition and sought to believe the best in others. In short, she was at home in her own skin; she was who she was – take it or leave it. And while she was not concerned with impressing others, she showed respect to others, treating them with dignity.

Our lives were greatly enriched through knowing and loving Aunt Jean. Personally, she probably didn't know it, or wouldn't say it, but she taught me several life lessons including the importance of honesty, humility and humor – qualities included in a life filled with grace and graciousness.

SCRIPTURE REFERENCES: Ruth 4:15; Job 12:12; Psalm 71:18-19; Psalm 92:12-14; Proverbs 16:31; Isaiah 46:4; 2 Corinthians 4:16-17.

QUESTIONS FOR REFLECTION AND DISCUSSION:
1. There is a need for us to take ourselves less seriously and to take God more seriously. How do you respond to this statement?
2. Give a look at Proverbs 17:22. What are the spiritual, emotional and physical benefits of joy and laughter?
3. What is your take-away from the statement, "If you're green, you're growing. If you're ripe, you're rotting?"
4. Contrast "life-long learners" and "congealers".
5. Read Psalm 92:12-14. What is some of the "fruit" you have experienced in the lives of older people?

PRAYER: O Lord, we thank you for those who though older in chronological years yet display an open mind and a positive spirit. We are encouraged by those who rather than becoming rigid and calloused in their perspective; instead, evidence and practice a flexible posture toward life. At all ages of our life keep us growing and not rotting. For Christ's sake. Amen.

WHY DO YOU SEE THE SPLINTER THAT'S IN YOUR BROTHER'S OR SISTER'S EYE, BUT DO NOT NOTICE THE LOG IN YOUR OWN EYE

-Jesus

(Avoid Projection and Casting Blame).

CHAPTER FIVE

OTIS

A Deep Hunger for God's Word

"Thy word is a lamp unto my feet and a light
unto my path." – Psalm 119:105

He was just about the last person I expected to sign up for the church Bible study we were soon to start. He was a quiet person who mainly kept to himself, and I never saw him very engaged in church-related ministries and activities. He attended worship most Sunday mornings, seated with his wife. Word was that she "insisted" that he be there, in the pew, beside her.

One week before our thirty-four-week Bible study was to launch, Otis approached me, "I would like to sign up for the Bible study class you're leading, if it's not too late," he stated. Truth said, the materials had already been ordered and we already had completed registration, with a full roster for class. But a voice in my mind seemed to say, "Let him in the class." And, so, we did. Otis became a member of our thirty-four-week class, intensely and relationally studying scripture together in community.

A WEEKLY BIBLE BUFFET

Otis displayed a hunger for God's Word like I don't think I'd ever witnessed before. Each week as we gathered around the table and opened our Bibles and our study manuals it was like a "smorgasbord" of scripture, or a "Biblical Buffet" from Otis' perspective. He feasted on the Word. He listened to our discussion intently. He took copious notes. He asked pointed questions. He was a "scripture sponge"! At the age of eighty-three, enrolled in his first and only Bible study, he wanted to learn and to receive his Creator's communication. He realized he did not have a lot of years left on this earth. He had neglected and rejected scripture study and contemplation in his past. But not anymore. No longer. Weekly, around the table with fellow believers, Otis feasted on the Word.

Weekly, through our gathered discussions, and daily through our assigned scripture readings, we were growing in our relationship with God and with one another. It thrilled my heart to watch Otis finding nourishment for the soul as he dug into the Word! St Peter instructs, "Like newborn babies, crave pure spiritual milk, so that by it you may grow up in your salvation, now that you have tasted that the Lord is good" (I Peter 2:2,3). That was Otis' status: craving God's communication. The entire class was inspired by observing him crave the Word. And it led us to take inventory, especially those of us who had participated in numerous Bible studies before. Did our hearts possess the same deep hunger accompanied with excitement which Otis displayed?

GOD'S WORD PRESENTED IN OUR WORDS

In Psalm 1, verses 1-3, we read: "The truly happy person doesn't follow wicked advice, doesn't stand on the road of sinners, and doesn't sit with the disrespectful. Instead of doing those things, these persons love the Lord's Instructions, and they recite God's instruction day and night! They are like a tree replanted by streams of water, which bears fruit at just the right time and whose leaves don't fade. Whatever they do succeeds."

The Lord's Instructions - God's written Word - the psalmist declares, presents the path of true peace, real happiness and abundant fruitfulness for Divinity's glory and honor. Instead of listening to disrespectful gossip and half-baked truths (heresies); and, instead of getting advice from misguided sources, the God-follower goes straight to the Source! Gratefully and graciously, Divinity has revealed God's self in human language! Talk about total Incarnation! God has come to us as Triune God – Creator (Father God, who continues to create); Redeemer (Jesus Christ, who is the Living Word among us); and Sustainer (Holy Spirit, who here and now brings comfort and guidance). Furthermore, through the mighty and mysterious work of the Holy Trinity, God's written Word is given to us in our own human language! God reveals God's will and ways to us on the pages of Holy Scripture in ways we may comprehend and receive. More importantly, God reveals God's self to us within the Bible, so that we may receive God into our hearts and lives. The Bible is more a divine love letter than it is a historical record. Through God's written Word we may know God and make God known. Through the Bible we are shown the way to redemption. Through holy scripture we are guided in the path of peace and reconciliation with God and with one another.

BEYOND INFORMATION TO TRANSFORMATION

I watched eighty-three-year-old Otis come to life while feeding on God's written Word. I witnessed a life changed before our very eyes, as this elderly man, reading and meditating on the scripture, was informed, but more importantly formed and transformed by the Holy Trinity working within his mind and soul each week as we gathered around the table feasting on the Word.

Three years after our Bible study class had ended Otis passed away. At his celebration of life all the members of the class sat together in two pews with an empty seat reserved in memory of Otis. In this worship service of death and resurrection we celebrated that Otis had gone to his eternal home to be with the One who created him, loved him, and had provided him the redeeming Word. This is the Word which Otis had thankfully and joyfully feasted upon, providing him with an abundant and eternal life!

SCRIPTURE REFERENCES: Joshua 1:8; Job 23:12; Jeremiah 15:16; Matthew 4:4; John 17:18; Colossians 3:16; 2 Timothy 3:15-18; Hebrews 4:12.

QUESTIONS FOR REFLECTION AND DISCUSSION:
1. Otis joined a Bible study class. What are some of the different dynamics between reading and studying the Bible by yourself and doing the same in a group.
2. These days, how would you rate your hunger and craving for the written Word of God?
3. Do you agree that God's written Word is a gift and miracle of Incarnation? If so, how so?
4. How do you respond to the statement, "God's written Word is a divine love letter?"
5. Reflect upon, and discuss, "The Bible is given for information, formation and transformation."

PRAYER: All-Powerful and All-Loving God, thank you for never ever leaving us alone! You have come to us, supremely in Your Son, Jesus Christ, our Savior and Lord. You have given us Your Living Word, Jesus, and you have gifted us with your written Word, the holy scriptures. As the Psalmist affirms, "Thy Word is a Lamp unto my feet and a Light unto my path." We celebrate, O Lord, your Word is a divine love letter to all humankind. We are not to worship the Bible, but we are to adore You who gave us this Word. May we take time regularly and frequently to read and to meditate upon Your Word, alone in silence, and, also within the community of faith. May we not only be informed by the scriptures, but may we be transformed for the sake of Your Kingdom on earth as it is in heaven. In Jesus Christ, the Living Word, we pray. Amen

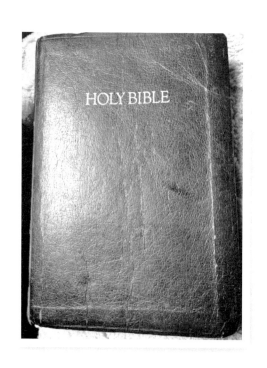

CHAPTER SIX

DAD

A Pioneer and Peace Advocate

"Life is a journey, make the most of it." - Unknown

My Dad, Elam Kurtz, or "Pop" as we affectionately called him, was a man of deep faith, many interests and enormous energy. I learned so very much from Pop. Most of my learning from him was not through his words, but rather through his actions and by watching his life. Dad was not much for small talk. At times he could be laconic and very reflective, yet not verbally expressive. I was, and am, a more verbal person than Dad, so there were times, I recall, when I really wanted him to converse more with me. Yet, that was not his style and method. As a result, more was observationally caught than verbally taught.

So, we often communicated through sharing activities together. He was good about spending time with all of us as family. We traveled as family - many trips and vacations - nationally and internationally. We played numerous and diverse games together – board games, card games, chess and checkers, and yard games, such as badminton, croquet, and horseshoes. Dad and I frequently hiked to several mountain summits in our home county. We rode off-road enduro motorcycles over many dirt sawmill roads. We even went on some bird-watching outings organized through CHAT (The Carolina Bird Club quarterly journal and organization, promoting bird watching, education about birds and the ecosystems they inhabit). He regularly took us to church, and he introduced us to cultural opportunities, such as music, theatre, museums and art galleries.

LIFE AS A DYNAMIC ADVENTURE, NOT STATUS QUO

Life was not boring with Dad. In fact, life was an adventure with Pop. I consider him a contemporary pioneer. He savored learning. He enjoyed new experiences. He possessed an exploring spirit. His travels took him to places such as, Russia, Israel, Europe, Haiti, and almost all the fifty United States. Yet, he did not need to leave his living room to travel and to explore. He explored geography, theology, medicine, philosophy, and a host of other topics and disciplines, through books. He would almost always have a book in his hands or one nearby. He taught me to love books and the joy of exploring life through reading.

Dad's pioneer posture and zest for learning led him as a young adult from operating the Pennsylvania family dairy farm to attending college, followed by medical school. Upon completion of internship at Case Western Hospital (Cleveland, Ohio), he moved to, and settled in, the northwest mountains of North Carolina. Here he and Mom raised our family and served the community through a busy and vibrant medical practice, and via various venues of volunteering – including church, mental health, Hospice and meals on wheels.

LIFELONG LEARNING

Dad was a life-long learner. He continued to learn literally until the day he died. On the day of his death, he did some reading and worked on a writing project. He kept growing. He never stopped learning. Pop's adventuresome attitude and love of learning contributed to his engagement in new experiences and relationships. For him, life was not an existence to be endured, but, instead, a joyous journey to be embraced and celebrated. His was a fluid life, juxtaposed to a frozen existence. Author Gail Godwin's words from "The Finishing School," as applied to fluid folks, aptly and accurately describe Dad:

"There are two kinds of people. One kind, you can tell just by looking at them at what point they congealed into their final selves. It might be a nice enough self, but you know you can expect no more surprise from it. Whereas, the other kind, keep moving, changing. They are fluid. They keep moving forward and making new trysts with life, and the motion of it keeps them young. In my opinion, they are the only people who are still alive. You must be constantly on your guard against congealing" (Viking Press, 1984; p.4).

A HUMAN CATALYST

Congeal is not word or concept I would ever associate with Dad (Similar to Aunt Jean, referenced earlier). Instead, I would select the word zeal. Pop possessed a zeal and a zest for life. And what he experienced and gleaned from life and living he desired to share with others. His learning was not only for himself, but to help others to become better. Dad was what I would describe as "a human catalyst," - offering up ideas, and suggesting relationship connections, to assist others in their life journey. I did not see, or appreciate, this connecting, catalyst characteristic of Pop in my younger years, but now, upon further reflection, I am amazed by, and grateful for, these altruistic attempts and accomplishments.

For example, on one occasion he connected me with husband-and-wife old time Gospel musicians (they were medical patients of his), with whom I eventually joined for a year of musical travels and performances.

This experience and relationship were life changing for me. It's like Pop could envision and anticipate how persons could possibly bring together their diverse God-given gifts and combine them to increase and multiply positive influence and lasting impact. Or, again, as to the catalyst and connecting quality, Pop, as physician, hosted fifty-six extern (contrasted with intern) medical students at his rural clinic during a thirty-year span!

Dad's passion and vision for serving others as a catalyst – teaching and assisting others in growing and learning – is expressed in his own words: "To teach students is a great joy. They, in turn, enjoy teaching other eager students. I plan to keep medical students in (my practice) year-round." Dad had learned and embraced the concept of being a teacher of teachers of teachers. Not only teaching but learning himself while doing so. Not only teaching other teachers (medical students); but teaching students who would then teach others. This led to exponential growth and to a continual ripple of influence. This was and is the proven path to having the maximum influence upon the maximum number of people for the greatest good.

THE MINISTRY OF MENTORING

Dad, with his vision, passion and catalyst-connection skills taught me so much about serving God and serving others. From him I was blessed to observe, and learn to serve through, the relationship skills of encouraging, enabling and empowering others to develop their God-given gifts and graces for Kingdom's sake.

Pop's mentoring style reminds me of the biblical Paul-Timothy relationship. It is like I can almost hear Dad's words through Paul's pen, ".... My dear son: Grace, mercy and peace from God the Father and Christ Jesus our Lord. I thank God….as I remember you in my prayers…. I remind you to fan into flame the gift of God, which is in you through the laying on of my hands…." (2 Timothy 1:1-6, selected phrases. NIV).

I will always be grateful to God for a dad who showed to me the path of following Jesus. And, for a dad who taught me the path of serving others. Serving and seeking shalom for all. He accomplished this, not so much through verbal expression but by way of vibrant example.

SCRIPTURE REFERENCES: Exodus 18:17-27; Proverbs 27:17; Acts 20:35; I Corinthians 11:1; Ephesians 4:11-16; Philippians 4:9; 2 Timothy 3:14.

QUESTIONS FOR REFLECTION AND DISCUSSION:
1. What are some ways we may keep from congealing in life?
2. How do you respond to the statement, "More is caught than taught"?
3. A human catalyst could be described as a person who works intentionally at connecting people for the sake of their human growth and for the betterment of society. Given this definition, who are some human catalysts you have witnessed in action?
4. Read and reflect upon 2 Timothy 1:1-6. What does this passage inform about the ministry of mentoring?

PRAYER: Nurturing God, we praise you for your continuing and guiding presence in our lives! You love and guide us in so many ways – your written Word, the scriptures; your living Word, Jesus the Christ, your Body, the church; your Comforter, the Holy Spirit; your handiwork, creation; and in a multitude of additional avenues of blessings. Thank you for the people you have placed in our lives who have loved, nurtured and mentored us so that we may be more fruitful servants for your kingdom's sake. As we have received, may we also share with others through intentional mentoring care. It is in Christ's name we serve and pray. Amen.

CHAPTER SEVEN

MOM

Lessons and Blessings

"Keep your eyes on the stars but remember to keep
your feet on the ground." -Unknown

At least two general topics, and qualities, come to mind when I think of Mom. Practical life lessons and sacrificial love blessings. She taught me a lot about both areas of living.

MOM'S PRACTICAL LIFE LESSONS

First, to her practical life lessons which I observed. Mom was raised during the Great Depression. Her family did not have a lot economically speaking. Yet, what they lacked in money, they made up for in their ingenuity. They were a family which was frugal. They grew much of their own food and even took some of their home-grown produce to sell at local markets, assisting family income.

Mom, or Orpah Mae Horst Kurtz, grew up as the only daughter of Elmer and Katie Horst, on a small family farm in the Reading, Pennsylvania area. She had seven brothers. She relates how, while growing up with all those brothers, she was a tomboy. She played ball, worked outside, and enjoyed being with the boys. I attribute this "background with the boys" for playing a major influence in Mom's better understanding of my brother and me. After all, she had firsthand knowledge and experience when it came to relating to testosterone-ridden beings! This likely gave her a head start on raising boys.

I recall times, growing up, when Mom would play ball with family and friends, in the front yard of our home. She would ride bicycles with us. And, for years, she rode motorcycles with Dad. She worked beside Dad in the vegetable garden, planting, cultivating and harvesting.

She taught me such things as how to garden and how to balance my checkbook. Again, from her depression-era upbringing, and from being raised in a family with little in terms of financial means, she had developed the skill of wise and careful budgeting. Mom knew how to pinch a penny and how to stretch a dollar. I affirm she could have written the book, "How to do much with little"! One year, for instance, she collected dimes. While planning a family vacation, one year out, she continued collecting dimes. On our trip she used the dimes for our fun money – ice cream, snacks and other treats along the way. It was truly amazing how those dimes multiplied, and purchased a lot of family fun, through her diligent and consistent saving practice.

While Dad, Pop, was more the dreamer of the marital dyad, Mom, Nanny, was more the planner. Pop would chase a vision. Mom would help to put legs under the dream so that some measurable progress could be assured during the dream chasing. She could share in dream-casting, yet to reach and fulfill the dream, "My goodness," I can hear her say, "You must have plans, and you've got to put feet under your dreams." I appreciate, from my perspective, mom and dad provided a healthy, functional balance between the dreamer and the pragmatic one.

Her high capacity as a person and her efficiency in practice, especially while multitasking, was something to behold! She seemed to possess boundless energy and an uncanny (Nanny) ability to plan and to coordinate.

MOM'S SACRIFICIAL LOVE BLESSINGS

Mom's economic background formed a frugality in her. Yet, even though careful with her stewardship of finances, she was a very giving and generous person. For example, my three siblings and I were fortunate to get orthodontic care because mama took us to our many appointments, with a significant number of miles travelling, and time to take, because there was no orthodontist in our small rural town. She invested in this travel, time and expending financial resources for all of us, providing us with a blessing and benefit of exceptional dental care. The kicker for me, as I reflect, was that mom, all her life had wished that her teeth were straighter!

Mama was a giver, a generous, kind giver. Many times, she inquired, even in her later years, while a resident in an assisted living facility, about how she could help with a need in the wider community when that need arose and was communicated.

I also was the recipient of mom's listening ear and counsel. As shared earlier, mom was a busy person, sometimes I perceived her as too busy. Yet we learned a way to connect and to share with one another. Our talking time became a regular tradition in the following manner. While mom would iron clothing in the basement laundry room, I would sit across from her on the basement steps, and we processed whatever the topic of the day might be. She became my sounding board at the ironing board.

While I valued these conversations with mom, for me lessons from mama were more caught than taught. She did not have to say a lot for I learned from watching her life – her dignity, her work ethic, her integrity, her treating others with respect, her manifest faith in Jesus. I consider myself fortunate to have had a mom who gave me lessons and blessings!

SCRIPTURE REFERENCES: Genesis 2:10; Proverbs 10:4, 12:24; Luke 6:38; 2 Corinthians 9:11-12; Galatians 6:2; Hebrews 13:16; I John 3:17.

QUESTIONS FOR REFLECTION AND DISCUSSION:

1. Who comes to mind when you think of a generous person? Provide a description of what their generosity looks like.
2. Some assert that there is a direct correlation between gratitude and generosity. Do you agree? How so?
3. Proverbs 12:11 shares, "Those who work their land will have plenty to eat, but those who engage in empty pursuits have no sense." A strong work ethic is important. What are the benefits of consistent hard work? What are the negatives of workaholism? How do we find a healthy balance between work and rest?
4. Reflect upon Colossians 3:23. According to this passage, what should be our primary motivation for our work?

PRAYER: Creator God, may we be reminded that work was a reality in the very beginning, in the perfect Garden. We have an innate, God-given need within us to work, create and to tend, as in "tend the garden." May we find meaning and joy in our work. May our work come from your calling, a vocation for service in your Kingdom. O Lord, enable us to work with diligence and purpose and lead us to times of renewing rest and re-creation endeavors, called sabbath. Lord, let us recall that even you, all-powerful God, rested from your labor. On the seventh day you rested. Thank you for the exhortation and example of a healthy life rhythm of work and rest. For the cause of Christ. Amen.

CHAPTER EIGHT

GRAY

"Heaven's Acolyte"

"Don't stop meeting together with other believers." -Hebrews 10:25

Missing church on Sunday morning was not something Gray ever entertained. To prove this commitment, he had a long train of over thirty, and growing, perfect attendance pins awarded for his Sunday School faithfulness. At the beginning of a new Sunday School year, while also celebrating the previous year, Gray loved to wear every one of his pins to church to show to all who had gathered. Whenever someone congratulated Gray on his great accomplishment he would break out in a huge smile and say, "I love it!"

SPECIAL NEEDS POPULATION HAS MUCH TO TEACH

Gray's speech was broken and unclear. Some would say he had developmental challenges as he had been born with Down's Syndrome. Yet, Gray had a strong commitment and a deep joy as he served Jesus by attending and helping in Christ's church. According to Gray, lighting the altar candles for worship each Sunday was his domain! After all, he was our appointed church acolyte. It was in print on our congregation's list of officers and ministry leaders, "Grey Bowman, Acolyte". He had served in this capacity for decades, and along with his perfect attendance pattern, no one dared dream of taking this serving role from him! Every Sunday Gray arrived early. He sat in the first pew, on the left side as you enter the sanctuary with his acolyte taper in hand. When the prelude began on the piano, Gray knew this was his cue to light the two altar candles. With great pride and dignity, the candles were carefully lit. Without fail he completed his mission.

One Sunday morning our congregation had a theatrical drama for our worship service. The altar table had been moved to the side so that the center platform could be employed for the presentation. Even though

Gray had been verbally informed of this change, he did not grasp the concept. And he most certainly did not agree with this different Sunday morning M O! Upon arriving his world was rocked! Immediately, he retrieved his acolyte taper, sat down in his seat in the first pew, and commenced crying. When we inquired what was wrong, he let us know through broken sentences and hand gestures that he intended to light the candles as usual. So, we placed the two altar candles on the altar table, now at the side of the sanctuary. We had the pianist play a prelude and Gray lit the candles. After this, when asked how he was doing, he responded with his big Gray-smile and his signature statement: "I love it!" It all ended well that morning.

EMPLOYING OUR GIFTS FOR GOD'S KINGDOM

Psalm 84 (10) affirms, "Better is one day in your courts than a thousand elsewhere; I would rather be a doorkeeper in the house of my God than dwell in the tents of the wicked." Gray certainly adhered to this gratitude philosophy of faithful presence. Every Sunday, lighting candles for Jesus. Serving without fail in the house of the Lord.

I once had a church member who faithfully and diligently cleaned the church facilities. She also had the wonderful gift of designing and producing extravagant altar displays for our worship center. When I asked her why she did her work with such care and detail she replied, "I consider myself a Levite." Wow! What a great sense of divine calling in the church!

In the Old Testament scripture, the Levites were called and appointed to serve God in the Holy Temple. They were specifically charged with caring for the maintenance and design of God's House. Their job descriptions included, but was not limited to, being custodians and musicians. They were some of the human agents who enabled worship to happen by assisting with logistical details. I imagine Gray would have made a first-class Levite! He showed up. He helped. He served in the house of the Lord. And, with his classic positive persona, "I love it!" he worshipped, and he helped us all to worship.

Perhaps one of Gray's favorite scriptures would have been, "I rejoiced with those who said to me, 'Let us go to the house of the Lord'" (Psalm 122:1). After moving from where Gray attended church, I learned one year that he had passed away. Certainly, Psalm 122:1 would have been a very appropriate epitaph for Gray's tombstone. Instead, a different epitaph was selected. It reads: "Heaven's Acolyte!" What a great fit! A fitting epitaph for a wonderful servant of God in God's House, who showed up early; taper in hand; lighting the sanctuary candles each Sunday, while proclaiming, "I love it!"

SCRIPTURE REFERENCES: Psalm 5:7; 27:1-14; 84:10; 122:1; Isaiah 56:7; I Corinthians 3:17.

QUESTIONS FOR REFLECTION AND DISCUSSION:

1. Many church researchers speak of the decline of worship attendance in our contemporary culture. Why do you think this has occurred? What might be the ramifications of this dynamic?

2. What might we learn from the special needs' population? Like Gray, how may they possibly serve in, and enrich, our gathered worship experiences?
3. What spiritual gifts and God-given skills have you identified in your life? How are these being employed for Christ's church and God's Kingdom?
4. The Psalmist declares, "I rejoiced with those who said to me, let us go to the house of the Lord.'" In what ways is worship of Divinity a "fit" for humanity?

PRAYER:

Heavenly Parent, each of us as your children, have unique gifts and special needs. May we employ them to your honor and glory. Thank you, O Lord, for the responsibility and the opportunity of gathered worship, as a community of faith. May our worship of You be done in spirit and truth. May we use our God-given gifts for the cause of Christ's community. And may we realize and experience the encouragement and joy that derives from gathered praise and corporate service, remembering that we are not alone in the Jesus journey. For when we each bring and offer our little, we affirm that God can multiply our offerings to grow and strengthen the Kingdom. For the cause of Christ may our worship be service and may our service be praise. Amen.

CHAPTER NINE

CLAUDE

Grateful for New Beginnings

"Once I was blind but now, I can see." -John Newton

Claude was not a member of our church family. But he was a citizen of our community. I initially got to know Claude through delivering meals-on-wheels to his home. At first, I left the meal on the porch. After a while, he came to the door, I handed him the meal and we exchanged a brief greeting with one another. Later, he invited me into his home to sit and converse. Through these times of fellowship and conversation we became friends.

BROKENNESS IN LIFE

I learned through our sharing that Claude had experienced a tough past and some very hard times. He was an alcoholic, yet by the time I met him he was living a life of sobriety. Nonetheless, the alcohol had taken a huge toll on his body and had made a devastating impact upon his relationships. He was divorced after a difficult marriage. His grown children would have nothing to do with him. There was an impasse, resulting from deep hurt and resentment in the family. Claude was attempting to reach out to his family to find forgiveness and hopefully some mending. However, the family had refused and rejected his overtures. And, truth told, Claude admitted and owned his errant ways in the past. He realized and confessed that he had let a lot of people, including himself, down along the journey of life.

GOD'S HEALING GRACE

Yet, there was new hope arising within Claude. He found Jesus. Or, better put, as Claude expressed it, "Jesus found me." In the words of a great hymn of the faith, "I once was lost, but now am found; Was blind but now I see" (Amazing Grace, John Newton). I was a firsthand witness to a transformed life. Claude was not only talking the talk (which is not unimportant), but he began walking the walk with God. He replaced his intake of alcohol with feasting on the Word. He located and met with a supportive 12-step recovery community. Worship of God became a living, loving relationship, instead of a misconstrued perception of Divinity as an angry, condemning, judgmental and harsh Heavenly Parent.

This joy-filled transformation did not happen overnight. It was a process. There was required time and trust. As for each and all of us, this discipleship transformation is a lifetime adventure and challenge. But Claude was invested in and committed to "a long obedience in the same direction." Claude took God up on God's Holy Spirit offering – the lifelong sanctification journey – seeking, through the Spirit's strength and guidance, to become more and more like Christ each day.

TAKING RESPONSIBILITY FOR SELF, NOT FOR OTHERS

Claude was learning and accepting that while he could not change his family members' hearts and minds, he would take responsibility for his life, including his words and actions toward his family. He would continue reaching out to them in respectful and kind ways, remembering that if there was ever to be reconciliation there would be mandated a two-way street requiring willingness and effort from all parties. He hoped and prayed for a reuniting, yet he had come to a point of relative resolve and serenity concerning the family. He could only offer his family his confession and his concern and care. But he could not force them to accept his offerings. That was beyond his control and exceeded his human capacity. In fact, the more he pushed and forced the relationship matter, the more the family resisted. So, he was learning, as difficult as it was, to leave the relationships in God's hands.

BREVITY AND SERENITY IN LIFE

He was also acutely aware of the brevity of life. When I knew Claude, he was in his early eighties. Add together his age and his rough lifestyle, including alcoholism, and his health had taken a huge toll. In addition, amazingly, Claude's body had endured twenty-two surgeries! He was weak. He was tired and worn.

However, amazingly, he was buoyant and encouraged in spirit. The peace that he had finally found, late in life, provided hope and serenity for eternity. God had given him, through God's grace, a calm confidence within his soul – a stability - that he had never known before. The words of St. Paul had become reality to

Claude in the center of his struggles and difficulties, "We do not lose heart. Though outwardly we are wasting away, yet inwardly we are being renewed" (2 Corinthians 4:16).

My final visit with Claude was to a hospital room where he was a patient, following his twenty-second surgical procedure. He made it through this surgery. Post-surgery, in his typical, classical Claude upbeat persona he reached out to me with as much vigor and energy as he could muster. As I entered the room, he greeted me in his raspy voice, "I'm glad to see you, preacher! How are you today?" As we shook hands, even while an I V tube was inserted into his arm, he gave me what felt like a vice grip clasp! We exchanged pleasantries. We visited for a few moments. We had prayer. I then left so that he might get some much-needed rest. That was to be the final time I saw Claude. He didn't make it to the discharge day, when he had hoped to go home.

GOD'S PROMISE OF PERMANENT PEACE

Instead, God called and discharged Claude to his heavenly home! The One who had created him; healed, restored and reconciled him, provided now a permanent place of peace and provision. A perfect place where the presence of Jesus surrounded him and nurtured him perfectly forever! Claude had contemplated and claimed this promise years before, as he read the words:

"Do not let your hearts be troubled. Trust in God; trust also in me. In my father's house are many rooms; if it were not so, I would have told you. I am going to prepare a place for you. And if I go and prepare a place for you, I will come back and take you to be with me so that you also may be where I am" (John 14:1-3).

We shared these assuring words of Jesus, from John's Gospel, at Claude's celebration of life service. His family members were in attendance, paying tribute. Paying tribute to a man who had experienced devastating brokenness in life's journey, yet who, because of his deep hurt and chronic pain, appreciated God's gift of reconciling grace probably more than most. Claude's testimony, in both word and deed, was summarized in John Newton's lyrics, "Once I was lost, but now I am found."

SCRIPTURE REFERENCES: Genesis 3:16-19; Psalm 90:5-6; Luke 6:37; John 14:1-3; Romans 3:9-20; I Corinthians 15:50-58; 2 Corinthians 1:3-11.

QUESTIONS FOR REFLECTION AND DISCUSSION:

1. What is your response to the statement, "We are all broken people, living in a fallen world"?
2. Read 2 Corinthians 5:17-21. What does this passage of scripture say about the healing of our brokenness and fallenness?
3. In our relationships with others, is it possible to try too hard? What are some examples of over-functioning in a relationship? How might this be dysfunctional and harmful?
4. What is your interpretation of the biblical passage which instructs, "Lord, teach us to number our days so we may gain the wisdom of God" (Psalm 90:12).

5. What is the "victory" to which I Corinthians 15:50-58 proclaims?

PRAYER:

Eternal, Life-Giving God, we confess that we have done what we should not have done. And, we have left undone what we should have done. Forgive us! Heal us! May we know your reconciling grace so that we too may proclaim, "Once I was lost, but now I am found!" As we experience your divine loving kindness, in our human response may we worship you with more passion and serve our neighbor with deeper compassion. We praise you that our eternal life, through you, begins here and now and never ends. For the cause of Christ, we pray. Amen.

ASSERTIVE SHARING AND ACTIVE LISTENING.

(Two Positive Communication Practices).

CHAPTER TEN

EMMA

Genuine Humility

"Blessed are the pure in heart: for they shall see God" -Matthew 5:8

During my graduate student days, I would often go to a nearby retirement community to sit and visit with some of the residents. I met a lot of wonderful mature citizens there, but one 94-year-old lady I will never forget. Her name was Emma.

Emma was blind and suffered from rheumatoid arthritis. Day after day she would sit in her room, in her wheelchair, listening to the birds outside her window or to recordings of scripture made available by her family. Despite Emma's varied limitations, over my many visits, I never heard Emma complain of loneliness or of impatience.

Each time I knocked on her door there was a welcoming greeting. She would eagerly ask what was happening in my life. After we had talked for a while, Emma would ask me to read from the Bible. Then we would pray together.

Whenever I visited Emma's room, I knew I had been in the presence of a very special person. Amid physical limitations, and some would maintain unfair circumstances, she evidenced a faith that was filled with hope and vitality. Emma was physically blind, but she had clear spiritual vision. Through her deep commitment to Jesus and her willingness to share with others she taught me to see more of life and more of the fullness of living.

IRONIC LIFE LESSONS

Upon reflection, I find it ironic that I, a sighted and fully mobile person, discovered a greater vision of life and living through an elderly blind woman, who lived most of her days confined to a small room in a nursing home. How easily we miss seeing and perceiving so very much in our earthly journey! If we are not mindful, we miss the majors by dwelling on the minors of life.

It was through a perhaps "least likely" person that I was provided greater, clearer vision. In terms of vision, who was really handicapped? It was paradoxical that a blind person assisted me in removing my blinders! Somehow, visits with Emma resulted in a better attitude and a healthier perspective within me, one of appreciation for the so-called small things in life. And with that renewed perspective came gratitude.

THE DANGER OF FALSE PRIDE

If we surmise that we can see things totally and clearly then we are self-deceived and on a dangerous path. Although our physical vision may be 20/20, our very best perception of reality and life is always limited. We require divine guidance and fellow humans' feedback to have a clearer, and truer, understanding. When we haughtily claim we have things figured out, that attitude defines and confirms our blindness. Because every one of us can learn from another. None of us possesses the complete picture or the total truth.

Jesus, one day when confronting the self-righteous Pharisees, a group who claimed that their knowledge was greater than others, states, "I have come into the world to exercise judgment so that those who don't see can see and those who see will become blind" (John 9:39). The Great Physician provided the prescription for the curing of blindness for self-righteousness.

HONEST INVENTORY IMPROVES VISION

Years ago, Methodist pastor and evangelist E. Stanley Jones, while engaged in mission work in India, would often host spiritual retreats known as ashrams. During the retreats Jones would sometimes invite participants to take part in a spiritual inventory exercise. He would ask the retreat pilgrims to write down a weakness or a problem in their lives. E. Stanley recounts that on a certain ashram, he requested that participants write down a particular problem or failure in their lives. A hand went up. When Jones acknowledged the man, the man asked, "Mr. Jones, what if you don't have anything to write down?" To which Pastor Jones quickly responded, "If you do not have anything to write down, then write that down, because that is your problem!"

We all suffer from myopia in life. We are short-sighted when it comes to viewing life. No one has complete vision. We all fall short of the glory of God. It is our human condition. We require help from beyond ourselves to see – help from God and from our neighbors. In the honest words of a beloved hymn, "Amazing grace how sweet the sound, that saved a wretch like me! I once was lost, but now am found; was blind, but now I see." Proper vision arrives through Providential guidance and grace. A right status and a right perspective not gained on our own but provided graciously by God.

So it was that a vision-impaired lady, Emma, taught me so very much about viewing life with proper perspective. My life has been indelibly influenced and positively impacted by a sight-impaired woman who saw consistently with eyes of faith.

Prior to graduating from divinity school and saying goodbye to Emma, I wrote a song entitled "Emma." I was able to sing this song to her before our parting of ways.

EMMA

Chorus:
Oh, I wonder Emma now what your eyes are seeing.
And I feel like you can see what my eyes are missing.
Though your eyes are blind, still you have such vision.
You show me what mere eyes will never see.

Verse 1
Sitting there in your room day after day
And hearing God's voice in a special way
You'll never know what you've been teaching me.
You'll never know how your life is reaching me.
(Chorus)

Verse 2
I came here today to bring you some cheer.
But every time I visit you, I know God is near,
For He's in your eyes, He's in your smile, and in your tears.
And I know that I've been blessed by just knowing you.
(Chorus)

SCRIPTURE: Deuteronomy 4:29-31; Proverbs 29:18; Isaiah 6:9,10; Isaiah 61:1; Acts 26:15-18; I Corinthians 2:6-16; Ephesians 4:17-18; Philippians 4:8; Hebrews 12:1-3; Revelation 3:18.

QUESTIONS FOR REFLECTION AND DISCUSSION:

1. Two people live with some of the same physical handicaps and disabilities. One withdraws from others and takes on a negative disposition on life that is limited and limiting. The other, while honestly facing their limitations, discovers ways to adjust, compensate and even thrive during challenges. From your life observations, what might account for these differences?

2. If we have the "eyes" to see, God may speak to us in unusual and even unlikely ways, perhaps using "least likely" persons to do so. Can you recall a "least likely" experience in your life?

3. Some maintain that false pride (hubris) is humankind's original sin. What might be the connection, if there is any, between false pride and spiritual blindness?

4. Reflect: What is a weakness in your life? Are you, perhaps, willing to share this with someone you trust? Maybe in sharing with another you would find the beginning of healing.

PRAYER: Jesus, Light of the world, shine on us! At times the world seems like such a dark place. Forgive us when we dwell upon dark thoughts, and when we dwell in darkness. Deliver us from blinding, poisonous pride and enable us to reside in, and to reflect, the light of your love. O God, as human beings our sight and perception is limited. We need You to guide us, to direct us, and to help us see the way, the truth and the life. Great Physician, we pray, please, for your providential prescription to restore and to enhance our sight. To the One who came to give sight to the blind, we pray. Amen.

CHAPTER ELEVEN

RUDY

A Wise Counselor and Confidante

"Without counsel plans fail, but with many
advisers, they succeed." – Proverbs 15:22

He had never taken a college-level Bible class, but he knew the scriptures. He had not attended seminary, but he could talk theology. He was not a trained therapist, yet he studied, diligently, human relations in God's university of life.

PRIESTHOOD OF ALL BELIEVERS

Rudy became my unofficial, informal therapist for a season in my life. He became a close friend and confidante. In classic Christian theology which affirms the priesthood of all believers, Rudy served the priestly role for me at various times. I have heard it wisely stated that every person needs a spiritual guide, a mentor and a therapist. In several ways, Rudy served all three of these roles for me during the years I visited with him. He was knowledgeable. He was approachable. And, above all, he was compassionate. He was a rare and gifted person who freely offered his wisdom and compassion to others.

THE NEED OF SOUL TENDING

As a person, and as a pastor, I greatly needed a confidante. Sometimes we as pastors can unfortunately take upon our shoulders the spiritual and emotional grief of others, while at the same time, neglecting to nurture our own heart and soul. This is a formula for burnout and burnup. We neglect our own emotional life at the peril of self and others. Without proper self-care, with the absence of healthy boundaries, we grow tired and worn. When proper rest, reflection and renewal are not a regular pattern for caregivers we are not enabled and empowered to care for others. This results in everyone suffering, both caregivers and care receivers.

In the presence of Rudy, I could rest. Instead of being a pastor "on call," I was a person free to be and free to be me. No pretension. With Rudy, the conversation frequently evolved out of open-ended questions asked of one another, which fostered and elicited reflection. These were not exam questions. They were not competitive, cornering questions. Rather, they were experienced almost as prompts, inviting us to discuss our universal human condition. Questions like, "How is it with your soul?" "What grief or loss are you experiencing?" "What is most pressing in your life right now?" "For what are you most thankful in this season of life?"

HONESTY WITH COMPASSION

Everyone needs a person with whom you can process life – the good, the bad and the ugly – in trust and safety. This trusted friend or mentor becomes a shelter for the soul, a safe harbor for the heart, which at times becomes stressed and strained from enduring the storms which inevitably arise on the sea of life during our sojourn on this planet. Dialog with Rudy was healthy and fruitful because of his deep level of care and his continual attention to honesty. He was practicing the scriptural instruction which states, "Tell the truth in love" (Ephesians 4:14-16). Rarely do we encounter a person who regularly integrates these two necessary practices – Tell the truth; and tell the truth in love. We can find folks who are loving, yet do not tell you the difficult truth to hear. Or we can locate people who are painfully honest, and "a pain" because they lack the critical love portion. To find an individual who will not hold back from you some needed, but tough, information; yet, at the same time, you know how much they care for you – this is a true friend!

Conversation with Rudy involved continually seeking truth in an environment of unconditional love and acceptance. I found a presence which provided sanctuary. I discovered a kindred spirit. Also, I experienced realness and transparency which created an environment conducive to mutual openness and vulnerability. Rudy would often set the tone and posture for our dialogs by relating very willingly some of the deep hurts and brokenness of his life. His openness in sharing about his personal journey freed me to reciprocate. My soul and my ministry were greatly strengthened through spending intentional time with this authentic Jesus follower.

REFLECTION, NOT PERFECTION

For over six years, twice a month, on Tuesday mornings, for two hours I made it a practice to meet with Rudy for a time of holy conferencing. I have no doubt, these "Rudy ruminations" helped to sustain and strengthen me for the work of ministry. I learned and discerned that Rudy regularly spent time alone in conversation with God. It showed. It radiated. I perceived that Rudy frequently practiced the spiritual discipline of "sitting at the feet of Jesus." That perception motivated me to learn more from this broken, yet beautiful, soul. Rudy's was not a persona of pretension. He would sometimes remark, when describing his life, "What you see is what you get, warts and all." What made him so real, and so approachable, was his not hiding his weaknesses and struggles. I perceived he did not display an attitude which sought personal attention and credit. Instead, his life and words pointed to Christ, his Savior and Friend. Rudy's M. O. was that of seeking divine reflection rather than claiming some sort of human perfection. He knew his weaknesses. He confessed his brokenness. His intentional alone time with Jesus enabled him to garner grace and wisdom, which he willingly shared with others.

The account is told of a young president of a company who instructed his secretary not to disturb him because he had an important appointment. The chairman of the board came in and said, "I want to see Mr. Jones!" The secretary answered, "I'm terribly sorry, sir, he cannot be disturbed; he has an important appointment."

The chairman became very angry. He shoved open the door and he saw the president of his corporation on his knees in prayer. The chairman softly closed the door and asked the secretary, "Is this usual?" And she said, "Yes, he does that each and every morning." To which the chairman of the board responded, "No wonder I come to him for advice!"

No wonder I came to Rudy for conversation and consultation. Rudy evidenced a daily walk with Jesus that was contagious. He possessed a non-anxious presence which set at ease those in his company. His open-ended, non-judgmental questions prompted and encouraged vulnerability leading to contemplation, catharsis and healing. My ruminations with Rudy were regularly rewarding!

SCRIPTURE REFERENCES: Proverbs 1:5; 11:14; 12:15; 19:20; 24:6; Romans 12:16; I Corinthians 13:1-13; I Thessalonians 5:11.

QUESTIONS FOR REFLECTION AND DISCUSSION:

1. What is your understanding of the concept of "The priesthood of all believers"? What are some ways Christians are called to practice the priestly role with one another?
2. Why is soul care often the last thing we humans tend to? What are some ways in which you practice soul tending?
3. Ephesians 4:15 instructs, "Speak the truth in love…." Where have you witnessed this instruction practiced?
4. Do you agree with this statement (Why or why not?): As Jesus followers, we are not called to perfection; rather, we are called to reflect the truth and love of Christ as best we are able. Reflection, not perfection.
5. Do you have a trusted friend or counselor, someone like Rudy, in your life?

PRAYER: God, thank you for giving to us your Counselor the Holy Spirit, who confronts, comforts and guides us into all truth. You, Lord, are the Way, the Truth and the Life. Forgive us when we go our own way, neglecting your perfect counsel. Thank you for working through the human counselors and trusted friends in our life, who care enough to hold us accountable to the life-giving pathway. As we are the recipients of good and wise counsel, may we then share the truth we have gleaned with love and compassion toward others. We praise you for your guiding Word, which is a lamp unto our feet and a light unto our path. In the strong name of our Good Shepherd, we pray. Amen.

CHAPTER TWELVE

NORMAN

A Mentor

*A mentor is someone who sees more talent and ability within you than
you see in yourself and helps bring it out of you. – Bob Goshen*

FINDING OUR NICHE IN LIFE

Everyone needs someone to believe in them. Someone to come alongside you and to relate and affirm the value and the potential they see in you. Life can be difficult, and culture may sometimes, with its negative, dog-eat-dog competition, bring us down, leading to deep discouragement. That is even more reason why and when we need encouragement. Perhaps from a close friend or mentor.

Norman was an encouraging mentor to me. As a young adult I was struggling to find my pathway in life. What was my purpose? What was my call? At the time I met Norman I was a high school teacher and coach. I found teaching to be a wonderful vocation. I had trained and prepared for what I thought would be a lifetime career. While I enjoyed teaching, there was a restlessness within that would not let go. Norman seemed to be a human catalyst who assisted me in discerning another calling. Little did I realize, until some enlightening words were issued from this valued mentor and friend, that ordained ministry would be in my future. I count Norman as a God-send friend and mentor at a critical juncture in life's journey.

DEFINITION OF MENTOR

The term mentor has had multiple definitions and applications through past centuries. Likely the word was first used in the field of literature, in Homer's "The Odyssey". The hero of "The Odyssey" is Odysseus,

King of Ithaca. Odysseus leaves home to fight the Trojan War. As he leaves, he leaves his old friend "Mentor" in charge of his household. Mentor, the one entrusted by the King, looks after the King's son, Telemachus – He becomes a father-figure, a teacher, a role model, and a trusted advisor to young Telemachus.

The term was used then, originally, for educating youth into adulthood. Mentoring was the guiding of children so that they might transition into mature, responsible adults for life's journey. While this child-guiding continues to apply to today's world, hundreds of years after the origin of the mentoring concept, the term became popular and was revived and revised in the 1970s. While the term still applies to youth being guided, it is also broadened in scope to include, mentoring, in an academic setting; in the workplace; for leadership development; and, as discipleship in religious communities.

In this more modern mentoring meaning, a mentor is one who comes alongside another with the intent of helping the mentee navigate life, through the mentor actively listening, and by reflecting and processing together. There exists a motivation on behalf of the mentor to assist in developing the mentee, who has ideally expressed desired goals upon which the two seek to obtain as a team. Mentoring, then, may be defined as, relationship with positive influence. As the relationship develops, the mentor assists in developing the potential -through expressed goals – within the mentee.

NORMAN, A MENTOR IN MY LIFE

Norman became that listening, reflecting relationship with positive influence for me at a time of restlessness and searching in my life. Norman was an ordained, practicing pastor in a parish within our community. I was part of a community Bible study which he facilitated. During this Bible study Norman would from time to time invite me to assist in leading the various sessions – leading a prayer, reading some scripture, and then, later, planning and facilitating a lesson. While I was unaware of it at the time, Norman was providing a training ground, a mentoring context, wherein I was developing skills for ministry leadership. After the Bible study sessions, in which I would share the leadership, he and I would process and evaluate how the sessions had gone. For example, how did I feel about the session? What went well? What could have gone differently?

One evening Norman's mentoring included arriving at a place of direct questioning. It was a moment I had not anticipated. In fact, at the outset, his question to me was overwhelming, bordering on the absurd and ridiculous! It hit me out of the blue. The setting? We were seated in a car on a snowy, cold winter afternoon. Of all things, we were headed to a nearby ski slope to do some skiing. Ironically, the roads were too icy to travel. So, we remained in Norman's neighborhood, transitioning into his living room. The question? As we sat and chatted that stranded afternoon, Norman had the gall to ask, "Michael, have you ever considered entering the ordained ministry? I have observed you in relationship with others. I have experienced your leadership roles in our Bible study. I have witnessed your love for Jesus and for people. Have you ever thought of being a pastor?"

After several moments of deafening silence, and my seeking to collect my thoughts and to gather my words, I responded: "Actually Norman, teaching and coaching at the high school level has been, and is, my calling. The education profession seems to be the right fit. No, I have not considered becoming an ordained pastor, leading a congregation. No, that hasn't entered my mind."

That was January of 1981. In August 1981, two very significant and life-changing events happened: First, I married the love of my life. Secondly, I entered seminary pursuing a Master of Divinity degree on the path to pastoring a congregation. A single and pointed question, presented out of a friendship relationship, led me to follow a pathway that included preparation for shepherding congregants in congregations.

ST. PAUL A MENTOR TO YOUNG TIMOTHY

Even though, at first, I was blown away by Norman's mentoring question to me, later I was humbled and honored that he saw, and named, some specific leadership qualities in my life. It was a gift. In this spirit of discernment of another's gifts, I'm reminded of St. Paul's mentoring relationship with mentee Timothy. At one point Paul writes to Timothy, "I have been reminded of your deep faith, which first lived in your grandmother Lois and in your mother Eunice and, I am persuaded, now lives in you also. For this reason, I remind you to fan into flame the gift of God, which is in you through the laying on of my hands. For God did not give us a spirit of timidity, but a spirit of power, of love and of self-discipline" (2 Timothy 1:5-7). Paul views leadership gifts and graces in Timothy's life. Further, he personally and intimately expresses these discernments to young Timothy. God, no doubt, used other persons (i.e., Lois, Eunice, etc.) and experiences to groom and grow Timothy into ministry leadership. Yet, it was Paul, at least as recorded on scripture's pages, who notices and names the gifts, graces and potential evident in Timothy's life.

To be sure, other factors were at play in my decision to enter the field of pastoral ministry, but very central in this calling discernment process was a mentor by the name of Norman. Norman saw something in my life which I did not see. He not only saw this "something", but he also named it. He spoke to me of his observations and shared his reflections of a possible divine calling in my life to pastoral ministry.

I-C-N-U

Some folks have termed this observing of, and sharing with concerning the gifts and skills noted in another's life, I-C-N-U. This acronym is a brief, condensed, succinct, and memorable way to say to a person, "I see in you." As I watch you; as I observe your life, I see these gifts, these abilities, these skills (customized and personalized to each person) which you possess. Have you ever considered these abilities which you evidence? I affirm these gifts and graces in your life and wanted you to know what I perceive.

What a wonderful way to bless another person! This should not be entered into lightly. It should not be shared without reflection and prayer. Yet, when we genuinely perceive gifts and graces in others, I submit this is our joyful duty to do so. This identification and sharing is person-edifying and, more importantly, Kingdom-building!

I thank God for Norman's mentoring in my life journey! He enabled and empowered me to see some leadership gifts and graces in my life, which at the time I did not perceive. He practiced the encouraging gift of "I-C-N-U." May we give thanks for the mentors in our life. Let us likewise offer the gift of mentoring to others, searching for, and affirming, God-given gifts in their lives.

SCRIPTURE REFERENCES: Deuteronomy 6:4-9; Psalm 71:18; Proverbs 27:17; Colossians 3:16; I Thessalonians 1:6-8; I Timothy 4:12; 2 Timothy 2:2; I Peter 5:3.

QUESTIONS FOR REFLECTION AND DISCUSSION:

1. Finding our calling in life is not always an easy process. What are ways and resources that can be used to help us discern our vocation?
2. One definition for mentor is, "Relationship with positive influence." How do you define the term mentor?
3. Norman is referred to as a mentor. Who has mentored you in your life? How were you mentored?
4. Read and reflect upon 2 Timothy 1:1-10. What are some of your take-aways concerning the Paul-Timothy mentoring relationship?
5. What gifts and graces do you perceive in a person in your life that you would be willing to share with them for their encouragement and blessing?

PRAYER:

Good Shepherd, thank you for the mentors you have placed in our life – people who have helped to guide and encourage us along the journey. Individuals who took the time to invest in us. (At this time may we pause and name some of those mentors before God, giving gratitude for their positive influence).

Dearest Friend, Lord and Savior, may we seek out someone with whom we may mentor through sharing our time and our life. As we have received, so may we give. Help us to carefully look for God-given gifts and graces in others – I-C-N-U – and encourage them by affirming their talents. (At this time may we pause and ask God to lead us to a mentee who may be needing guidance and encouragement). For Christ's cause and Kingdom's sake, we pray. Amen

CHAPTER THIRTEEN

JIM

Sing the Song Placed Within You

God put a new song in my mouth, a hymn of
praise unto the Lord. – Psalm 40:3

Music was a part of who he was. It brought solace to his soul. It provided a salve for his pain. It gave joy to his heart. Music was certainly one of his gifts, and Jim for sure spoke the language called music.

SOOTHING THE SOUL THROUGH SONG

The Eternal Composer had placed a song within his heart and life, and Jim sang it! Life was a great and blessed adventure for him. He worshipped his Creator. He worked hard in his career. He cherished his family. He drank deeply of life – treasured friendships, traveled often throughout God's great world, while enjoying hunting, fishing, golfing, and many other interests and hobbies in life.

Yet, as wonderful as all these experiences were, nothing seemed to soothe his soul and speak to his heart, like that of music! Music was his go-to. Music provided him with a centering. Music connected him to God and to people. How he loved to sing!

SING THE LIFE-SONG PLACED WITHIN

How tragic to leave this world having never ever sung the song the Creator has placed within each of us! The song placed within us by the Divine Singer may be any number of spiritual gifts, natural skills, or God-placed graces. Singing is only one of the many gifts God has placed within humankind for the purpose of praising God and serving people. It is our human condition to persistently seek, to gratefully find, and to passionately "sing" the gift – the song – which Providence has purposely placed in our persona.

One of life's languages which connected Jim and me was the language of music. It was a common interest and truly a passion of our hearts. I count music as one of God's precious and treasured gifts. Songs have a way of succinctly and melodically enabling us to give expression to that which is universal and relatable to our human condition. Music provides an avenue for offering collective praise unto our Creator. Think of it, many voices blending, singing the same words at the same time to the same God! What a gracious and powerful gift, lending itself to corporate praise and worship!

No wonder the Psalmist declares, "Sing to the Lord a new song; sing to the Lord all the earth" (Psalm 96:1). Or, again, from scripture we are encouraged, "Let the word of Christ dwell in you richly as you teach and admonish one another with all wisdom, and as you sing psalms, hymns, and spiritual songs with gratitude in your hearts to God" (Colossians 3:16). Singing is one wonderful way in which to worship God, and an avenue through which we may encourage one another.

SINGING IN THE MIDST OF SUFFERING

I was inspired by Jim's passionate singing. When listening to him sing one could see that he sang from his heart. It was not merely making vocal sounds. It was not robotically voicing the lyrics. Instead, it was a communing with God. It was a time of connecting with friends. This was particularly impressive and noteworthy as Jim in his mid-80s was still projecting and holding whole notes.

The odds of Jim living, let alone singing, were stacked against him. He had survived a major heart attack, which left a significant portion of his heart damaged. Prior to the cardiac episode, he suffered a ruptured aneurysm. His body was battered. His medical history of treatments and procedures was voluminous. His daily pill box contained a plethora of prescription medications, mandatory for making it. It was difficult for him to walk. Sometimes it was hard to talk, let alone sing. Yet, with a determined mindset, and persistent effort, somehow Jim kept on singing.

A SIGNATURE SONG

He kept on as an active member of our church choir. On one occasion, I inquired if he would be willing to sing a duet, during a worship service, with me. He graciously agreed. We both sat on stools in the chancel area on a Sunday morning and sang the hymn, "Just A Closer Walk with Thee." From that day forward that hymn became our signature song. Whenever we encountered one another, prior to exchanging greetings, we would break out in song, together singing, "Just a closer walk with Thee. Granted Jesus is my plea."

Jim's health soon took a downward turn. What was already tough, became even tougher to endure. He began having falls. He required oxygen to be administered daily. He no longer left the house. His wife, Carolyn, lovingly and dutifully looked after him as best she could. She, of course, needed to run some errands and take care of everyday responsibilities.

I began to visit Jim, in his home, almost every Tuesday morning. It provided time to sit and talk with him, while Carolyn could have a respite and go out for a little while, at least. If the weather allowed, we would sit on their patio, drinking coffee, looking at the majestic trees bordering their backyard, listening to the birds in song. When we were not seated in the outside space, we would find ourselves in Jim's favorite sitting room, surrounded by his many books and collection of arrowheads, which he himself had discovered on various landscapes throughout the United States.

Yet, no matter when we met, or where we sat, patio or parlor, before speaking we sang our signature song. Regularly on Tuesdays, for almost fourteen months, upon arrival in each other's presence we sang, "Just A Closer Walk with Thee." And upon departure, when I would leave his home, each time we would sing the first verse of "Amazing Grace." These two hymns formed the musical bookends to many treasured visits together.

ONE LAST SONG

Nearing the end of those fourteen months of musical greetings, Hospice was called in to provide care and comfort for Jim's final days on earth. I still went to see Jim on Tuesdays. It was hard for him to issue a sound. It appeared singing was over for him. On a chilly February afternoon, Carolyn called and informed me that Jim was slipping fast. The Hospice nurse said it would not be long now. I went right over to their home.

I sat by Jim's bed. I talked to him. He did not verbally respond, but his eyes opened, and he turned toward me. I told him I loved him and that it was okay for him to leave, he had fought the good fight, and Jesus would receive him into his arms on the other side. After a few moments we had prayer, Jim, Carolyn, the Hospice nurse and me. As I got up to leave the room, it suddenly hit me, I had not sung our song. I began singing, "Just a closer walk…" As I sang the word "walk," Jim's voice, raspy and weak, began singing along, "…Walk with Thee. Granted Jesus is my plea." Then he was silent and seemed not to be coherent. Carolyn and the nurse stated these words of the song were the only words he had uttered in more than twenty-four hours!

That evening Jim made his exit from this earth. For Jim, the "closer walk" became the utmost intimate walk with his Savior forever! I have no doubt that he is now singing, truly to his heart's content, and to the glory of his Savior, in the heavenly choir.

SCRIPTURE REFERENCES: Psalm 33:1-3; 96:1-4; 150:1-6; Isaiah 42:10; I Corinthians 14:15; Ephesians 5:19; Colossians 3:16; Hebrews 2:12.

QUESTIONS FOR REFLECTION AND DISCUSSION:

1. Consider a worship service without music. Describe your thoughts and feelings about a music-less service.
2. Identify a "song" placed within you by our Creator. What gift, skill or talent, or music about which you feel passionate, is a part of who you are?
3. What might the singing of songs through times of sorrow and suffering do for the human soul?
4. Take out a song book, or search the worldwide web, for one of your favorite songs. Reflect upon the lyrics, or possibly sing this selection. Why is this song special to you?
5. With all the strength he could muster from his Hospice bed, Jim sang one last time the words to his signature song. Does this final scene, perhaps, say anything to you about the human psyche and soul?

PRAYER:

Creator God, we are created in your image - imago Dei - which includes our deep desire to create. You have created humankind with diversity. Many gifts, one Spirit. May we employ our God-given gifts and talents to fulfill our calling in life; to fill us with joy, and to further your Kingdom on earth as it is in heaven. Loving Lord, may we sing the song that is placed within our lives before we leave this earth. For your praise and purpose, we pray. Amen.

IF YOU'RE GREEN YOU'RE GROWING. IF YOU'RE RIPE YOU'RE ROTTING.

-Ray Kroc

(Maintain an open posture of learning from the other).

CHAPTER FOURTEEN

PAUL AND RACHEL

Teaching the Word

Make disciples of all, teaching them to observe
all that I have commanded. - Jesus

During the mid-1950s a husband-wife team in Pennsylvania answered the call to go to the hills of North Carolina and plant a Mennonite congregation. Paul and Rachel packed up their earthly belongings and moved their family to an unfamiliar place, with an unknown future. Reminds me of the biblical account of Abraham and Sarah, going without knowing.

A MINISTRY COUPLE SERVES

As a young child, my family and I, along with many others, had the blessing of having Paul and Rachel as our ministerial couple. For several years Rachel was my Sunday School teacher. After completion of one class, I remember Mrs. Mast, and the congregation, presented me, a young teen, with a Bible. Rachel nurtured me and many in the Christian faith walk. She also had the gift of Christ-like hospitality by making others feel welcome in her presence and several times inviting us into their home for delicious food and warm fellowship.

Paul was our preacher for many years and in addition he also taught discipleship classes for those considering joining the church family. I recall, as a thirteen-year-old, I was the only one in the class, and yet he took the time to meet with me once a week, for several weeks. He wanted to make certain that I was aware of the basics of living the Jesus-following life.

Because our congregation was a small membership church, and was unable to pay a fulltime salary, Paul was what is often referred to as a bi-vocational, or "tent-making," pastor. In addition to pastoring, Paul was a farmer. He milked cows, harvested crops and tended to souls. Every Sunday morning, he drove a van over many miles of rural dirt roads, picking up people and bringing them to worship at the Meadowview Chapel. Then, after a couple hours of Sunday school and worship, Paul would load up the van and take the folks back home.

ASSIMILATED INTO APPALACHIAN AREA

At first, the mountain indigenous folk wondered about this strange new couple, coming from Pennsylvania – they dressed differently, they had a different accent, and they were representing a different denomination for Ashe County. Why did they come to the Appalachian Mountains? Why were they starting a congregation deep in a hollow of North Carolina? What was a Mennonite anyway?

However, as the years, and even decades, passed by, Paul and Rachel and the family found themselves more and more integrated in the culture and accepted by the local population. Their neighbors saw the care displayed. They witnessed the good that Paul and Rachel were doing. After a while they were assimilated into the southern mountain culture and lifestyle. They had passed the local litmus test, and they were accepted as residents and neighbors.

A MINISTRY MELTING POT

The church Paul and Rachel pastored became a melting pot of Baptists, Presbyterians, Mennonites and the unchurched from the community. More trust was developed as folk realized this church plant was not a cult. The Mennonites were Bible-believing people with emphases upon peace, simple lifestyle, and a discipleship theology which emphasized following Jesus, for example, by seeking to adhere to his Sermon on the Mount teachings. The Anabaptists, of which Mennonites were included, taught a radical obedience to Jesus Christ, not only in talking the talk, but seeking to walk the walk. Discipleship was, and is, a Mennonite mantra. Radical obedience to Christ was a clarion call. Anabaptist ancestors in Switzerland during the 16th century had paid dearly for placing their faith allegiance above government support. Some were even burned at the stake as martyrs. "Martyrs Mirrors" is a printed historical rendering of the sacrifice and commitment to the Christian faith evidenced by many persecuted Anabaptist believers. Even while facing torture and death at the hand of their oppressors, many refused to recant and to deny Jesus as Lord.

From this Mennonite history, theology and practical divinity, evolved a people who affirmed God's Kingdom must hold primary allegiance, before any humankind kingdom, even to the extent of practicing nonresistance. The Anabaptist subscribe to the teaching that as Creator, God has given life, and only God has the right to take life. Therefore, they will serve their country through, for example, voluntary service through humanitarian channels. But they refuse, as conscientious objectors, to bear arms against another human being. Radical obedience to Christ, and to Christ's teachings, should be evidenced daily in one's life, including life and death matters.

The local population evidenced the consistency, and peace-making, caregiving ways, in the lifestyle and service of Paul and Rachel. Their lives did not yield, nor did they claim, perfection. Rather, they yielded reflection – Christ's life and love shining in and through them. Their pointing to Jesus as Savior and Lord provided authenticity to their ministry. As St. Paul shares, "For we do not preach ourselves, but Jesus Christ as Lord, and ourselves as your servants for Jesus' sake. For God, who said, 'Let light shine out of darkness,' made his light shine in our hearts to give us the light of the knowledge of the glory of God in the face of Christ" (2 Corinthians 4:5,6).

God employed Paul and Rachel to help shape a faith foundation in my life, and in the life of many others. Because of their willingness to sacrifice, leaving their home and many of their kin and moving to an unknown, rural and some would say, "a deserted, mountainous area," lives were touched and transformed for God's Kingdom. Because of their Christ-following commitment, lives became established and rooted in Jesus Christ.

Sixteenth-century Catholic priest, Menno Simmons, who founded the Mennonites, has a scripture verse inscribed on his tombstone in Friesland. It reads, "For no one can lay any foundation other than the one already laid, which is Jesus Christ" (I Corinthians 3:11).

On Christ the solid rock we stand, all other ground is sinking sand. Jesus is our Rock and our Redeemer. In a culture which is shaky and shady, Jesus Christ offers a firm footing, a sound foundation for our lives. I am grateful to God for witnesses, such as Paul and Rachel, who helped to form foundational faith within me and others. In the words of an old hymn,

HOW FIRM A FOUNDATION

How firm a foundation, O saints of the Lord,
Is laid for your faith in his excellent Word!
What more can he say than to you he has said
Who unto the Savior for refuge have fled?

Fear not, I am with you. Oh, be not dismayed,
For I am your God and will still give you aid.
I'll strengthen you, help you, and cause you to stand,
Upheld by my righteous, omnipotent hand.

Throughout all their lifetime my people shall prove
My sovereign, eternal, unchangeable love.
And then, when gray hair shall their temples adorn,
Like lambs they shall still on my shoulders be borne.

The soul that on Jesus hath leaned for repose,
I will not, I will not desert to his foes.
That soul, though all hell should endeavor to shake,
I'll never, no, never, never forsake!

SCRIPTURE REFERENCES: Deuteronomy 6:7; 32:2-3; Psalm 1:3; Psalm 119:105; 2 Timothy 2:15; 2 Timothy 3:16; John 16:13; Ephesians 3:17; Colossians 2:6-7.

QUESTIONS FOR REFLECTION AND DISCUSSION:
1. Recall someone in your life who has sacrificed so that you, and others, might benefit and grow. Perhaps journal, or discuss with someone, about their positive influence.
2. Who, perhaps, has helped you better understand God's written Word? How did they help you?
3. On the Christendom Tree there are many denominations. Mennonites, for example. What might be the benefits of a multitude of denominations? What might be the downside of so many?
4. How do you respond to the Anabaptist position on non-resistance?
5. What forms the foundation of your life?

PRAYER: O God, our Rock and our Redeemer, thank you for those you have placed in our lives who have taught us your written Word, and pointed us to your living Word, Jesus the Christ. May we plant our lives firmly upon the firm foundation that we may be strengthened and not shaken when the winds of life blow. In the name of the One who is our anchor and refuge, even Christ, our Lord. Amen.

CHAPTER FIFTEEN

JOHN and JOAN

Exemplifying Grace and Generosity

Grace to you and peace from God our Father and
the Lord Jesus Christ. – Philippians 1:2

Sometimes folks experience relationship "chemistry" difficulties with their in-laws. I, however, was blessed to win the jackpot on the in-law matter. In my recollection, I pretty much hit it off with John and Joan over the years and through many experiences. After all, they did me an awesome favor: they raised a fantastic young lady and permitted me to marry her! Following forty-three years of marriage (as of this writing) with Karen, I affirm that after Jesus, she is the best thing that ever happened to me! I certainly was grateful to have John and Joan going to bat for me when I was courting my now bride, because for a while there were some other fellows in the running! But, with the good Lord, some old-fashioned perseverance, John and Joan's advocacy, and Karen exercising her free will, I lucked up! In fact, Joan would frequently say, "Michael is my favorite son-in-law." That made me feel so confident and good! However, as I studied that statement, it came to my realization that I was also her only son-in-law.

GRACIOUSNESS TOWARD ALL

My father-in-law, John, exhibited grace and graciousness toward all. Although he was a "successful," what some would term a high-achieving pastor, and for a portion of his career served as a district superintendent, an administrative leadership role in his denomination, he was not stodgy or haughty in his approach to life and to others. Instead, he presented an open, humble spirit and a wonderful sense of humor. He did not take himself, or life, too seriously. Because of this open, approachable persona, folks were drawn to John. Even if you disagreed vehemently on a topic or issue with John, his open, genuine and grace-filled, including a positive sense of humor, qualities could disarm you and invite you into a civil dialog. John had some one-liners, that if they did not cause you to chuckle out loud would at least bring a smile to your face. Lines like, "Hope you had a good trip, see you next fall," when perhaps you nearly took a stumble. Or "T B or not T B, that is congestion." Or, again, when speaking of a Manhattan shirt, "I would not have had this shirt if a man hadn't given it to me." Not everyone appreciated his punny humor. I, for one, did. And his one-liner legacy lives on in his family.

THE WORLD IS MY PARISH

His engaging and winning ways, affirming folks for who they were, enabled John's ministry and relationships to be widespread and diverse. John rubbed shoulders with society's poor and disadvantaged, as well as the wealthy and aristocratic. He was an avid advocate for the civil rights of all, while at the same time an active member of several so-called status-oriented civic organizations. He could be right at home with a group of community clergy from many different denominations or after the meeting adjourned take off his sport coat and necktie and play a game of pickup basketball with his children (and in-law!) in the family's backyard.

He served, and was at home, in the small membership, rural congregations he pastored, as well as in the large membership urban churches where he had also led as pastor. He was not exclusive or parochial in his ministry. In the spirit of John Wesley's affirmation, "The world is my parish," John reached out in ministry and mission to the larger surrounding community, helping to develop ministries of social justice, caring for the least, the last and the lost. His ministry style incorporated an evangelical, heart-warming, personal walk with Jesus, combined with a social outreach. Out of an authentic encounter of, and conversion to, Christ, a lifestyle including acts of justice and words of mercy was manifest. John put feet to his faith. This was living into the spirit of St. James, as he writes, "Faith without works is dead." John's faith, I affirm, was alive!

GENEROSITY OF HOSPITALITY

John and Joan were a ministry team, evidence of a faith that was very alive and vibrant. John's engaging graciousness and Joan's amazing generosity of hospitality fed many souls and many stomachs! On occasions I witnessed my mother-in-law (Joan) bringing a van loaded full of food to a ministry conference, whereupon she prepared the food, served a meal, and invited decades of delegates attending the conference to come and feast at their small cabin on the hillside of a beautiful lake. Looking back, this was an amazing and astounding hospitality task to pull off! In fact, we would sometimes jokingly reflect, "Joan, like Jesus, was feeding the five thousand on the hillside, overlooking the lake!"

Joan took Christmas gifting to a new level. Especially when the grandchildren came along! Her gift tradition was to lay out each person's Christmas gifts on a piece of furniture, couches and chairs in their living room. The gifts were unwrapped and laid out for the recipient, and all, to behold. Walking into the living room on these Christmas morning occasions was a bit like taking a stroll through the Sears and Roebuck Christmas Wish Book Catalogue of yesteryear! All year long she had been purchasing gifts with each person in mind, buying unique and personally tailored items for everyone. Joan was a generous giver.

Together, John and Joan served several congregations, various surrounding communities, and even participated on a plethora of mission teams around the world, spreading the good news of Jesus Christ in word and in deed. In one community where they served, they were instrumental in instituting a crisis ministry organization to feed and clothe those in need. This much needed and much utilized outreach continues its ministry today and has even grown to offer not only food and clothing, but also free dental and medical care and rehabilitation resources for those caught in substance abuse and addiction.

HEALTHY INTEGRATON OF EVANGELICAL AND SOCIAL ACTION

The above, as well as other ministries and outreach efforts, evidenced the ecumenical spirit and social justice focus of John and Joan. Above all and in all, their evangelical heart-warming Jesus emphasis was the driver of their missional outreach. I witnessed in them a healthy integration of a personal piety grounded in their Savior and Lord, Jesus the Christ, through regular practice of spiritual disciplines, while at the same time, evidencing the practice of social activity rooted in God's call to justice and mercy. For instance, evening family altar time was practiced, which included a reading of scripture followed by everyone in attendance bowing on their knees in the living room for a time of prayer. And, again, the next day would very likely include taking a meal to a shut-in and volunteering time at the local ministry crisis center.

Their scripturally guided worldview, their Christ-centered upbringing, and their commitment to following Jesus through gospel teachings, reinforced through a Wesleyan window, kept their evangelical, social action faith and lifestyle believable, balanced and biblically based. The graciousness and generosity shared by John and Joan helped to make me a better person, and positively impacted many others for the cause of God's Kingdom!

SCRIPTURE REFERENCES: On Graciousness – Leviticus 19:34; Matthew 6:14-15; Matthew 18:21-22; Luke 6:37; Ephesians 4:32; Colossians 3:13; I Peter 3:8. On Generosity – Psalm 112:5; Proverbs 11:25; Proverbs 22:9; Matthew 10:42; Luke 6:38; 2 Corinthians 9:11-12; Hebrews 13:16; I John 3:17.

QUESTIONS FOR REFLECTION AND DISCUSSION:

1. Graciousness may be defined as, "the quality of being kind to and considerate of another." Who has been a gracious person in your life? How did they display graciousness to you? What impact, if any, did it have upon your life?

2. What do you think John Wesley meant by his often-quoted line, "The world is my parish"?

3. Generous hospitality frequently involves food for the stomach and food for the soul. That is, in our gathering together and breaking bread something more happens than only eating physical food. Read John 6:5-15. Following the reading reflect upon and discuss how this feeding by Jesus fed physical hunger and potentially spiritual appetites?

4. John and Joan exemplified a lifestyle which integrated both an evangelical heart-warming faith, along with practicing social justice, reaching out to the least, the last and the lost. What are ways we may practice keeping this essential balance of sincere piety and consistent outreach activity alive in our lives for Kingdom's sake?

PRAYER: Gracious and Generous God, thank you for your amazing grace and your generosity experienced in the spiritual and physical gifts which you lavish upon us as your children! We thank you for those who reflect and share your graciousness and generosity with us. These people have greatly encouraged our lives through their kind and caring ways. May we be inspired to share with others the graciousness and generosity we have received so that your Kingdom may be furthered on earth as it is in heaven. In the name of our gracious and giving Lord, Jesus Christ, we ask. Amen.

CHAPTER SIXTEEN

GRANDADDY CHRISTY

Steady and Reliable

Let your yea be yea, and your nay be nay. – Jesus

SIMPLICITY AND INTEGRITY

Grandaddy Christy, my wife's paternal grandfather was a mountain man through and through. Years ago, when we resided in the piedmont area of North Carolina, and he was in the Carolina hill country, once in a great while we brought him to stay with us. Two nights away was his limit. He did not like being away from his hill-surrounded home. He greatly missed his beloved mountains. When we'd take him back home, driving westward toward the hills, he would say, upon our first view of the mountains, "Finally, something to rest my eyes against!"

Granddaddy was a simple man from a simpler time. Yet, while simpler, they were hard times. He worked for many years for the Nantahala Power and Light Company, laying lines across the mountain terrain. He knew difficult labor, living off the land (he always raised a garden), and he practiced the love and care of community and neighbors. Granddaddy helped folks in need, supported civic fundraisers and town improvements, and showed up in the pew every Sunday at the Andrews Methodist Church. He was part of the Builder's or Greatest generation who sealed deals with handshakes and always kept their word! You could take his word to the bank! He kept his word. Even at the hometown hospital

Once, while an in-patient at the local Andrews Hospital, located about a half mile from his home, he asked the doctor if he could be discharged. The doctor replied, "No, not yet. Possibly in a couple days if you keep improving." John informed the nurse on duty that he was going home. He commenced putting on his clothes, walked out the front door of the hospital, and strolled back to his house. Two days later he was out in a stream fishing for trout! One of his very favorite hobbies was fishing. He especially loved fishing Little Snowbird Creek, near Robbinsville, N C. A person was blessed if you got to go fishing with Granddaddy on Little Snowbird, because he knew that creek like the back of his hand. He and his fishing buddy, Vic, likely fished in those waters hundreds of times. I count myself fortunate to have fished with Granddaddy on the Little Snowbird more than once Each time I caught more fish than I ever did elsewhere and on my own. The reason for this success? Granddaddy knew and directed me to the fishing "hot holes."

TENDER-HEARTED and TOUGH-SKINNED

John, Sr. was also the consummate southern gentleman. He opened doors for ladies. He delivered a firm handshake for both a greeting and to close a deal. Every time that I was in his presence he was the same person. Steady. Kind. Non-anxious. Grateful. Never flashy. Always friendly. Tender-hearted, yet tough when he needed to be (Think of running power lines over rugged mountain terrain and raising two boys). Easy-going, but determined (Think of leaving a hospital without discharge papers). I aspire to be more like Granddaddy, tender-hearted and tough-skinned. That is, remaining resilient in relationships, remembering, when perhaps a slight or a hurt comes your way from another, that hurt people, hurt people. It's probable that their unkind comment or action derives from unhappiness within themselves. It is unlikely that the negativity is about you. Recalling this likely reality enables us to display mercy to the other (while not disregarding appropriate accountability as called for) while keeping our heart (compassion) alive and active toward others. As Ephesians 4:32 instructs us, "Be kind to one another, tenderhearted, forgiving one another, as God in Christ forgave you."

THE GIFT OF PLAYFULNESS

John also displayed a contagious sense of humor. He was a kid at heart. Granddaddy never lost the playfulness and a sense of awe that a healthy child displays. Thankfully, he did not allow the seriousness and sophistication, which sometimes arrives with adulthood, to overtake his appreciation of, and zest for, the simple pleasures and beauties of everyday living. His inner child was affirmed and nurtured. He nurtured this inner child through things such as, regular admiration of the Creator's awesome artwork, watching his garden grow, eating ice cream sandwiches with family, taking a drive through the countryside, and collecting windup toys. Granddaddy greatly enjoyed watching the windup toys moving across his living room floor – a train engine, a wobbly duck, and a flipping monkey. He watched these with a childlike fascination and belly-shaking laughter, which was beautiful to behold!

Granddaddy was a good, God-honoring man. Just being in his presence made you a better person. I also owe him a debt of gratitude for presenting his only granddaughter at the church altar to be my wife! At the ripe old age of eighty-one, he escorted Karen down the aisle of the sanctuary, so that she and I might enter the status of matrimony. However, prior to walking Karen down the aisle, and before the wedding ceremony began, he located me in a room behind the chancel area. He approached me with a big smile, extending his worn, but still sturdy hand. As he firmly clasped my hand, I will never forget his words: "Welcome, son, to the army that has never won a battle!" I have thought about his words many times over these decades of marital life. And you know what? He was right! His words were prophetic! Or, as I can hear him saying, "Truer words were never spoken through false teeth!"

I give thanks for Granddaddy's life. He represented his "builder" generation with dignity and integrity. Like many of that era, they were dependable, reliable, and you could, indeed, take their promises to the bank!

SCRIPTURE REFERENCES: Exodus 34:6, Psalm 33:4, 105:8, Proverbs 11:13, 14:5, 17:22, Matthew 4:19, 5:37, Luke 16:10, Ephesians 4:32, Colossians 3:9,10, Hebrews 13:5-8, I Peter 3:15, I John 2:5,6.

QUESTIONS FOR REFLECTION AND DISCUSSION

1. If you had to pick three reliable people in your life, who would they be?
2. Are you a dependable person? When you give your word to do something, can others count on you?
3. Consider scripture texts, such as Proverbs 11:13, 14:5, Colossians 3:9,10. Following the reading of these Bible verses, list some qualities and characteristics of a trustworthy person.
4. God alone is ultimately trustworthy. Reflect upon, and give thanks for, God's faithful love and care. Study texts such as, Exodus 34:6 and Hebrews 13:5-8, to guide your reflections.
5. Granddaddy maintained and nurtured his inner child through the practice of playfulness. A contagious joy was visible and palpable while watching granddaddy laugh and play, even into his nineties. How do you embrace and express your God given inner child? As you reflect upon and discuss the topics of laughter and playfulness, give Proverbs 17:22 a read. When is the last time you had a letting go, belly-shaking laugh?

PRAYER: Creator God, you are the One who created for our enjoyment and awe, creatures such as giraffes, hippopotamuses, kangaroos, and the like. You must certainly have a sense of humor and a divinely playful spirit! Thank you, for the childlike portion of our being, given us at our beginning. Forgive us when we have denied and squashed that healthy and necessary part of who we are. Jesus, you played with the children, partied at celebrations (even turning water into wine), and always remembered that you are God's only, holy Child, in whom your Heavenly Parent is well pleased!

No doubt, your sense of joy and a playful spirit emanated from the security derived from the loving, watchful care of your perfect Heavenly Father. Lord, we are grateful for your trustworthiness! You always keep your word, and you promise to always keep us in your hands. May we constantly trust you, as a small child is totally dependent upon the nurture and care of responsible earthly parents, lending protection and provision. In our Lord's name we pray. Amen.

CHAPTER SEVENTEEN

MY KAREN

Noble Character

"A wife of noble character who can find?" -Proverbs 31:10

EARLY RELATIONSHIP HISTORY

We met in elementary school. She was six years of age, I was eight. We were raised in the same small town. Occasionally, as we got older, we would end up in the same neighborhood field for a game of pickup football. Karen was the first draft pick. Tall, long arms, fast on her feet, tomboy spirit (raised with three brothers, what choice did she have?). She made the ideal wide receiver.

FIRST DRAFT PICK!

As kids, neither of us had any clue that one day we would be one another's first draft pick! After sixth grade, Karen moved away from our town. I had not seen her for nine years. After those years of MIA, she returned to our mountain community as a ministry intern with several rural churches. A mutual friend of Karen's and mine informed me that Karen was back in our county, and he wondered if I would contact her? I did. I'll never forget that phone call. I re-introduced myself to her. We remembered each other from our growing up years. I asked her if we could catch up on our lives and would she go out to dinner with me for a time of conversation? She said she would. We set up the time and the restaurant. A few minutes later I got a call back from Karen. She stated that she had agreed to our plans too hastily and had not thought things through. She was in a relationship with another guy, and she felt it was not right for her to go out with me. However, she offered an alternative plan. What if I came and ate dinner with her and her roommate, who shared an apartment with her? I was all about that! Plans were arranged. I was very excited about the two of us being reacquainted after all these years.

I showed up at her apartment. As I rang the doorbell, my heart probably going into arrythmia, Karen opened the door. As I saw her, I'm certain my heart raced even faster! Wow! She looked nothing like I recalled. She was no longer the lanky, tomboy who ran passing routes on the neighborhood makeshift gridiron. What a beautiful young lady she had become! She invited me into their apartment. Her roommate, Doris, and she had prepared a delicious meal for our enjoyment. We shared food and fellowship at the table, and during the meal, I became more and more drawn, not only to Karen's outer attractiveness, but also to her inner beauty.

MERCY. PURITY (KAREN, MEANING "PURE ONE"). AUTHENTICITY.

To be honest, I was disappointed that Karen was involved in a steady dating relationship. However, I was encouraged that she did not completely close the door to me. We did have an enjoyable meal together. Later that evening, we learned that we both played guitar and liked to sing. We spent over an hour singing songs together. As I looked back, I was hooked! I was ready for a relationship. Yet Karen wasn't at the same place. Truthfully, I respected her straight forwardness with me and her integrity as concerns being upfront and honest about her relationship status. That is who she is, a person of honesty and integrity.

Gratefully, she did arrive on the same "relationship page" that I was on, eventually. It took some time. And some airplane travels to Omaha, Nebraska (where she served for two years as a church and community worker), from my residence in North Carolina. With time and intentionality, significant relationship progress was made. In addition, over a two-year courting season, we made a lot of long-distance phone calls, mailed many handwritten letters, and sent up many prayers. During the summer of 1981, I drove to Omaha, the two of us spending months in a steady dating relationship. Then we drove back together to North Carolina. In late August of that same year, we were married, then moved to Durham, N.C., where I began studies at Duke Divinity School and Karen found employment.

MERCY GIFT

In our over four decades of marriage, I have learned much from Karen about Jesus following. She exhibits unconditional love. Her acceptance of, and affirmation toward, me and others illustrate and manifests divine love. She perceives and believes the best in others. From the first time we were reacquainted, that evening at mealtime and going forward, I have felt her belief in, and support of me. This unconditional love and belief in me from Karen have generated confidence and encouragement that has bonded us together for all time. I only hope and pray that I have reciprocated for her sake and for her good.

As strong and as true as Karen's exhibition of unconditional love is, I would testify that her greatest gift is that of mercy. Mercy here is defined as loving kindness. Tender loving care. Karen displays and practices a deep compassion with heart and hands reaching out to the down-and-out and disenfranchised. Mercy-giving is both planted and cultivated in Karen's persona. I affirm that the Creator has given her the spiritual gift of mercy (nurturing, caring, showing kindness), and she continually develops and deploys this God-originated gift. Mercy, divinely gifted to, and grafted into, her is received, embraced, and enthusiastically and generously shared with others.

Mercy in Karen's life, as for each of us, speaking metaphorically, results from both the paint and the paintbrush. God, the Master Artist and Designer, offers and provides the paint in one's life. Then, as co-creators through God's gracious invitation, we, humanity, become the paintbrush through the decisions, choices, and actions we make and take. Divinity takes our life and uses it for Kingdom's sake, in ways we often cannot see or perceive. Yet, through amazing grace, God will bless even our mess! Even though we paint and color, outside the lines, somehow God can and will transform our messing up into a blessing for others and for us. Our lives, in God's hands, through God's mercy, become broken and beautiful masterpieces for the Divine Designer! I affirm and celebrate, Karen has embraced and employed her God-provided gift of mercy. This is evidenced by simply being in her presence.

Thank you, Karen, for the journey together! You are a great blessing to me and to so many! Bless you for receiving, developing and sharing the loving kindness gift with which our Heavenly Parent has gifted you. "Blessed are the merciful, for they shall receive mercy." May you always know our Lord's tender loving care. I love you always and forever!

SCRIPTURE REFERENCES: Lamentations 3:22-23, Psalm 100:5, 145:8, Micah 6:8, Matthew 5:7, 9:13, Luke 6:36, Colossians 3:12-13, James 2:13, I Peter 1:3.

QUESTIONS FOR REFLECTION AND DISCUSSION:

1. Whether romantic or platonic relationships in your life, recall and recount what drew you to a significant other relationship in your history. What have you learned, and perhaps incorporated into your life because of this other?

2. Mercy may be defined as, "loving kindness." Read and reflect upon some listed, or additional, scripture verses which speak of God's mercy toward humankind. How have you experienced God's mercy?

3. In what ways have you experienced and received mercy from another person in your life? Perhaps take some intentional time to remember these mercy words and actions and give thanks for the persons who showed you mercy.

4. Pause and ponder: To whom might God lead me to demonstrate mercy this day?

5. Read and study James 3:8-13. What does this passage teach us about mercy?

PRAYER: Merciful Lord, your loving kindness is better than life. We, in our sinful rebellion, deserve your wrath, but instead you give us your grace. Amazing, undeserved grace. We have done that which we should not have done. And we have not done that which we should have done. Please, O Lord, hear our prayer. Forgive our transgressions.

We thank and praise you for mercy! We would be forever lost and condemned without it. We are also grateful, God, for those in our life who have extended mercy to us. As we have received mercy, so may we share that same undeserved mercy with others. May the justice of God and the mercy of Christ be evidenced in our living. In the all-powerful, all-loving name of our gracious God we pray. Amen

AGREE TO DISAGREE
AGREEABLY.
					-George Whitefield

(Keep an open mind;
Keep a relationship).

CHAPTER EIGHTEEN

ANNA and JOSHUA

Joy Persona and a Strong Leader

And a child shall lead them. – Isaiah 11:6

If mindful and vigilant, we parents may learn a lot from our children. Upon reflection, I'm profoundly reminded of how parenting provides a powerful providential lesson in learning more deeply of God's, our Heavenly Parent's, love for us as His children. To watch the birth of your child; To attempt to grasp the awesome miracle and the holy mystery of life as you hold a newborn baby in your arms; Then, observing your child's total trust and absolute dependency upon the parents' nurture and care, can surely call us to a healthy remembrance, and a holy humility, as we recall our human total dependency upon God's love and care.

Our children taught me much as they grew up, and now grown continue to influence and instruct my life. From Anna, our youngest, I have learned more about authentic joy and empathic relationship qualities. From our firstborn, Joshua, I have learned more deeply about steady perseverance and compassionate leadership.

TEARS OF JOY

It is said that newborn babies do not shed tears at birth. Our Anna shed tears during her first moments of entrance into this world! I witnessed the tears rolling down her tiny, just-come-into-the-world face. Along with her mom and the attending physician we noticed. We were amazed. "Something special about this child," the doctor affirmed. Of course he was right. Looking back, with the benefit of now knowing Anna's persona, I believe newborn Anna's tears were tears of joy. Tears of empathy. And tears of a deep sensitivity and great compassion for all living beings.

EMPATHY DISPLAYED

It is no wonder that Anna has pursued a career path as a teacher of children. Even when she herself was a young child she was drawn to nurture and care for little ones. Then, through her teen years, she was often sought out by families to babysit their children. This was followed by her work as a childcare educator, a vocation she has continued to cultivate and to practice. She is a teacher and an advocate for the little ones in our world. The innocent. The ones who have no voice. Those who are totally dependent and completely reliant. Anna, and others following this teaching vocation, are helping to touch, teach and train young lives so that they may mature and grow into wholesome human beings and responsible citizens of society, for the betterment of God's world. Anna channeled her tear-producing empathy and her love for children into educating little ones.

In a culture where rock stars and professional athletes capture multi-million-dollar contracts for simply playing games and performing concerts, teachers, like Anna, fulfill a role which develops young minds and positive character with permanent value. Yet, wrongly, these educators work for a relatively small amount of financial reimbursement. Tragically, culturally we have our priorities confused. Teaching and nurturing children is way more important than athletic games and musical concerts (as fun and entertaining as they are!). Teachers are helping to shape souls and lives. What a high call! What a necessary and noble profession, educating children and youth! No wonder Jesus said, "Let the children come unto me, for of such is the kingdom of God." Thank you, Anna Rebekah, for your contagious joy and encouraging empathy, which continues to teach me and many others!

RESPONDING TO THE CALL

When Joshua was three, on many Saturday mornings, while Karen needed a well-deserved break from the weekday routine, I would walk with our son down the quarter-mile dirt road to our church. I would wrap up a few pastor preparations for Sunday morning in the church office. Then, often, the dad-son ritual would go something like this: I would get out a folding chair and place it behind the pulpit. Whereas Josh would then climb up and stand on the chair and begin leading worship. I was to be part of the congregation, so I quietly took a seat in a pew. Josh would lead the entire service. He shared announcements pertaining to the parish. He had the ushers lift the offering. There was a song, which I was invited to, and delighted to, sing along. Then, he presented a sermon and concluded with a benediction. We then put away the folding chair followed by walking home hand in hand. I consider that holy time! Sacred son and dad time in the sanctuary.

At three years of age Joshua was leading worship and preaching the Word! At age twenty-three Josh was enrolled as a student at Duke Divinity School, preparing for a path into ordained ministry. His mom and I, a clergy couple, had encouraged him to consider doing anything but pastoral ministry if possible. He taught middle school students for one year, employing his undergraduate degree in the field of education. Then, he declared and affirmed, "I cannot run from God's call to ordained ministry. I sense the Lord's call in this direction. I'm going to seminary." That was what we had hoped to hear, "I sense the Lord's call..."

PERSEVERANCE PRACTICED

Like Joshua from the pages of scripture, Josh is a leader with vision, passion and compassion. He desires to give God his very best. He will not tolerate mediocre. He continually strives to creatively and positively give Jesus, and those he serves, the best that he can offer.

Joshua's passion for Jesus, and his perseverance for Kingdom service, are two of his practiced gifts and qualities. I have been instructed and encouraged by his "stick-to-itiveness"! It is engrained deeply in his persona. For example, while in college, playing on the men's varsity basketball team, he struggled with a nagging injury, a torn meniscus in his right knee. Yet, he would not quit. The team trainer would drain the knee, where fluid would collect, then wrap the knee, and Josh continued to play games and finish the season for the team. That consistency, dependability, and perseverance, on the basketball court, is manifest throughout his life and ministry. Whether on the basketball court, in the courts of praise, or engaged in mission outreach to and with the culture, Josh offers his best, realizing that God will take that which he brings and multiply and enhance it through divine grace. Joshua, thank you for serving Jesus through serving others, and for teaching me leadership lessons in "a long obedience in the same direction."

SCRIPTURE REFERENCES: Nehemiah 8:10; Psalm 47:1; Proverbs 17:22; Matthew 5:9, 18:2-4, 19:14; Romans 15:13; Galatians 5:22; Proverbs 19:17; Matthew 9:36; Romans 12:15; Galatians 16:2; I Samuel 5:8; Romans 11:29; Ephesians 4:1; I Thessalonians 5:24; 2 Peter 1:10; Romans 5:3-5; Ephesians 6:18; Philippians 1:6; Galatians 6:9; Hebrews 12:1; James 1:12, 5:11.

QUESTIONS FOR REFLECTION AND DISCUSSION:

1. What, if any, differences do you perceive between the terms "happy" and "joy"?
2. Empathy could be simply defined as, "relating to and caring for another." Some would describe empathy as seeking to walk in another's shoes. How important, in your opinion, is empathy in a relationship? Why or why not?
3. Christian theology affirms that every believer has a call to ministry, both generally through sharing the gospel in word and deed, and a specific call related to the reception of God-given spiritual gifts. What do you perceive as your Divine-given calling and spiritual gift(s) for serving God and others in this world?
4. Life is sometimes hard. Challenges and difficulties are a part of living. Read and reflect upon James 5:7-11. What does this passage say about perseverance, and how might this text relate to your life?

PRAYER: Holy Heavenly Parent, thank You for creating us and calling us as Your children! Through Your grace and guidance, we are nurtured and directed all the days of our life. Your wise word informs us we must become like a child to inherit the kingdom. That is, we must trust and depend upon You. When we heed your instruction in our attitude we become child-like, but not childish. That is, totally dependent upon You, our Heavenly Parent, but not self-centered and petty. As Your children, allowing Your light to shine in and through us, may we respond to Your call with joy and perseverance for the sake of Your Kingdom. Thank you for the children in our lives – little ones and grown – who influence and impact us for the cause of Christ. As Your word relates, "For a child shall lead them." In our Lord's name we pray. Amen.

83

FORGIVENESS IS THE OIL OF
ALL RELATIONSHIPS.

-Anonymous

(Forgive as you have been forgiven).

CHAPTER NINETEEN

MORRIS WALKER

A Non-Anxious, Supportive Presence.

Don't worry about anything; instead, pray
about everything. – Philippians 4:6

Growing up, I aspired to be a high school teacher and coach. In 1977, Mr. Morris Walker, principal of one of my hometown schools provided me an opportunity to fulfill my goal, hiring me to teach English and coach boys basketball at the secondary level.

DO WHAT IS RIGHT

Morris is a kind and patient person. I observed him treating teachers and students alike with respect. You could tell that he had entered the education field for the sake of students' betterment and advocacy on behalf of faculty and staff. Morris' son, Chuck, once stated, "Dad was not a complicated person. He had a simple philosophy which he taught us and which he lived. His number one rule: You do what is right. And in his educational career, that simple and single philosophy translated to, you do what is right for the student."

A CALM SPIRIT

One of the primary ways in which I observed Morris' patience and kindness was through his consistent non-anxious presence, especially in times of stress and crises. For example, students at the school where he served as principal would at times display acting out behavior, triggered by their frustration and anxiety. Mr. Walker had a way with his calm demeanor and steady presence to often calm the agitated student. His calm spirit set the posture for the entire school – students, faculty and teachers. As is the case always, the leader sets the tone for the entire organization and group. Mr. Walker's daughter, Mitzie, shares, "One thing I especially appreciate about dad is this: He was always the same. He provided a sense of calm, even-keeled, level-headedness. That helped many times to give me a sense of calm, sometimes in the middle of some chaos."

I recall my own high level of anxiety when as a newly hired coach I was required to operate an activity bus to sometimes drive athletic teams to contests. I completed my test drive, navigating successfully the turns, the parking and operating all the internal bus controls. Then it came time for me to back the bus into the bay in the school garage. I checked the mirrors. I went back slowly. Then it happened! I had improperly angled the bus while backing and heard the shrill noise of the bus scraping an unseen metal support beam located in the middle of the darkened garage. This rookie coach had placed a racing stripe on the side of a school activity bus! I was worried. I called Mr. Walker. He arrived a little while later. I was braced for the worst. I was prepared for a verbal lashing. Instead, Morris, studied the scrape on the bus, looked at me without any condescension, and stated, "Coach, it's okay. This has happened before to this bus. You are not the first. Besides, this is the old activity bus, and it has about finished its service. Don't worry about this incident. Next time, when backing, just watch out for the post." What a relief! His gracious approach and great patience shown me amid a bad mistake left an indelible impression upon me. It also provided me with a lesson: No matter what the situation, even when you may be very anxious, keep your cool, stay calm, and demonstrate respect to another, especially when they have messed up and perhaps already feeling down on themselves. The late Coach Jim Valvano was patient and quiet after his basketball team had lost a game by a large margin. A team reporter, who had observed this patience of Valvano, asked him later why he did not berate the team for their poor performance. His response? "Players don't need to be reprimanded after a loss, they're already feeling bad enough. I choose to lecture them after a big win, lest they become overconfident."

Morris' non-anxious presence proved very helpful when he was coaching a high school state championship basketball team, prior to becoming a principal. Coach Walker, while starting as an assistant coach on this team became head coach due to the lengthy and severe illness of the original lead coach (Coach Rose). Again, his consistent, reliable leadership greatly helped the players who were dealing with many challenges and obstacles. With Coach Rose gravely sick and with the basketball team facing several opponents where they were considered underdogs, the stakes were high. No doubt anxieties were elevated. Overwhelming obstacles can easily and quickly breed angst and anxiety. Morris Walker, now head coach, provided the steady persona required. The Coach's steady temperament, along with talented and determined team members, enabled this team to accomplish something very special and unique to happen – the winning of a state championship!

A PATIENT PERSONA

Morris' mantra, "Do what is right," along with his patient persona was greatly put to test when his wife Katy began showing signs of memory impairment at the relatively early age of sixty-four! Just when a married couple begins to plan for and to reap and enjoy the fruit of their labor, in the season of retirement, an unforeseen loss and grief occurs. How would Katy be cared for? Yet, for Morris, there was no question about it. He would look after his soulmate and care for her every day. This he did, lovingly looking after her daily needs. This was his method of operation as long as he could physically maintain. The medical community assessed and intervened after years of his undivided care for his lifelong partner. Seeing Katy's condition and observing the toll taken on Morris, the attending physician said in no uncertain terms, "Mr. Walker, it is time now for you to place Katy in third party care, in a memory care facility, for her sake and for yours." For the final year of her life Katy resided in professional memory care. Yet, every day Morris would visit his teammate for life. Katy was lovingly cared for, and Morris had no regrets.

MORRIS A MENTOR

There exists a close bond between Morris and me. Years ago, when Katy faced a tough and sobering medical diagnosis, Morris and I went jogging. As we jogged along, Morris requested that I pray out loud, as we ran, an intercessory prayer for Katy. I did. The rest of the run we talked and cried, hoping for a good medical outcome. Since that experience something special has connected us. Decades later Morris would ask me to preside at Katy's funeral, which I was honored and humbled to do.

Morris has been, and is, a treasured mentor in my life. His steady ways, his dependability, and his ability to look for and to see the best in others are all admirable characteristics I wish to practice. He has positively influenced and impacted so many people, and I am one of those influenced. His life mantra, "Just do what is right," coupled with his non-judgmental and non-anxious persona, are traits I desire to emulate. I affirm Philippians 4:8 could well be a signature scripture for Morris' life, "Whatever is true, whatever is noble, whatever is right, whatever is pure, whatever is lovely, whatever is admirable – if anything is excellent or praiseworthy – think about such things." I give thanks for Morris Walker, a strong mentor and positive influence in my life.

SCRIPTURE REFERENCES: Proverbs 21:2-4; Matthew 5:10-12; Galatians 6:9; Colossians 3:23-25; Psalm 56:3; Isaiah 41:10; Philippians 4:6-7; 2 Timothy 1:7; Colossians 3:15; Proverbs 15:18; Romans 8:25, 12:12; I Corinthians 13:4; James 5:8; Proverbs 27:17; Colossians 3:16; I Thessalonians 2:8; I Peter 5:5-7.

QUESTIONS FOR REFLECTION AND DISCUSSION:

1. Morris' motto for living is, "Just do what is right." What are your guides and possible mantras for making the right choices and decisions in life?

2. Anxiety is prevalent in our culture. Peace and serenity are antidotes to our anxieties. How may we experience peace amid chaos?

3. Recall a person who demonstrates a non-anxious presence. How do you describe their persona?

4. Read Romans 8:22-27. How may we practice patience when dealing with the complexities and difficulties which come our way in life?

5. Mentors are guides who "come along side," to encourage us. Who has been a mentor to you? In what ways have they encouraged you?

PRAYER: O God, our Help in ages past, our Hope for years to come, how we thank you for your gracious guidance in our journey of life. Lord, we express our gratitude to you for the mentors you have placed in our lives – those who enlighten, encourage and exemplify to us, through integrity and through their calm demeanor when facing anxiety. Our spirits have been lifted, and our joy increased because of these who have given of themselves to us. May we openly receive another's gift of their presence and guidance. And may we also reach out to provide mentoring guidance and encouraging care to another. In the name of Jesus, our Good Shepherd. Amen.

CHAPTER TWENTY

GRANDPA AND GRANDMA KURTZ

A Life of Discipleship and Simplicity

Do not conform to the pattern of this world but be transformed
by the renewing of your mind. Romans 12:2

Growing up, I always looked forward to the summer season, when I would often get to spend a week or two on Grandpa and Grandma Kurtz's dairy farm in Pennsylvania Amish land. I'm certain I got in the way more than I helped, when it came to farm chores. Nonetheless, I was always met with a gracious greeting and wonderful hospitality whenever I arrived from our North Carolina mountain home.

THE IMPORTANCE OF FAMILY

Looking back now, I observed and gleaned much about faith and family values from watching Grandma and Grandpa. For starters, they were married seventy-three years! They evidenced a deep covenant commitment to one another. Together they purchased and operated a large dairy farm, raising the cows and shipping tons of milk to a local distributor. It was quite the enterprise, including family sweat equity, managing hired hands and the buying, operating and maintaining of heavy farm equipment employed for plowing fields and cultivating crops used to feed the cattle.

Their marital union also included the birthing and raising of seven children – five sons and two daughters. Together the family ran the farm, completed household chores, attended worship every Sunday at their local Mennonite Meeting House, engaged in family morning devotionals each day, and when time would allow, they enjoyed some family table games together. It was a simpler time. Yet it was a harder time attempting to keep the family farm going, especially during the Depression Era.

THE WAY OF INTERDEPENDENCY

Faith, family, friends and farm work were the focus of their corporate life and identity as a family unit. These priorities were also the focus of their larger local community. Farmers helped one another from barn raisings to crop harvesting to sharing food at table together. The local community provided a place and a people in which to belong. Together neighbors shucked corn, quilted cloth squares, shared farm hands, loaned farm equipment and attended church together. Life was not designed to be lived in solitaire, siloed from one another. These were community-minded folk, living in solidarity with one another, not in isolation. Working hard, and carrying one's own share of the load, was a very important value; yet, also of great importance was that of assisting and helping one's neighbor in time of need. As the Book of Galatians, chapter six affirms, there is a dynamic and delicate, yet important, balance between independence for self and dependency upon others. "Carry each other's burdens, and in this way, you will fulfill the law of Christ…And each one should carry their own load" (6:1-10). This can come across as a biblical contradiction. Possibly appearing upon first reading as a direct contrast. Yet, upon further and deeper reflection, rather than a contradiction there is here presented a realistic and healthy relationship principle and practice. Namely, avoid fierce independence and stay away from parasitic dependency through the practice of interdependency. Functional interdependency in simple terms affirms, "In my time of need I lean on you. In your time of need you lean on me." Herein, we help one another without hindering each other.

Grandma and Grandpa had navigated and learned a M O relationship of learning from, and leaning upon, one another. Grandma Kurtz had a gift of teaching. Growing up, she had her sights on being a schoolteacher. She gravitated toward books and reading. While the formal, professional path of school teaching never panned out, the farm and family took precedence, yet Grandma had her own in-house class, as she imparted much knowledge and guidance to each of her seven children.

While Grandma had the gift of teaching, Grandpa was a lifelong learner. Homework assignments did not come as naturally or easily to Grandpa as they did to Grandma. In fact, I learned that during their teen years, as school classmates, Grandma helped Grandpa with his schoolwork enabling him to pass classes. Grandpa was not a particularly fast reader, yet he was persistent about it. One indelible picture I have of Grandpa is his kneeling on the living room floor with the newspapers spread out before him. Every day he would read in this manner for a long period of time, keeping informed of current events. He likewise would read biblical and theological periodicals with this same focused posture and motivated interest.

Grandma possessed a cheery disposition and a playful spirit. She loved to recite riddles and to relate funny stories accompanied by hearty laughter. Grandpa displayed a more reserved and stoic persona. I experienced him as kind, yet more measured than Grandma was. My take was Grandpa provided more along the lines of guidance and prudence for life, while Grandma offered the adventure and nurture for living. Together they seemed to bring a balance with their complementary styles which taught and impacted all of us as intergenerational family members.

AUTHENTIC PIETY

I find three overall lasting life lessons yielded through the examples of Grandma and Grandpa Kurtz. They are lessons of piety, simplicity and charity. By piety here is meant a positive spiritual term and description. It includes showing reverence for God and respect for the children of God. It has been described as the gift of reverence for life. One of the means through which I witnessed Grandma and Grandpa practicing reverent piety was in family altar time. Some call this family devotions. This time of reverence and worship included some traditional Christian spiritual disciplines, or practices – such as a time of reading scripture, a time of singing hymns and a time of prayer, usually kneeling on the living room floor as prayer was shared. As a young boy, these altar times felt a bit awkward, and besides there were other activities in which I was ready to participate. However, this devotional time was a household priority, and it was how your day began when you visited with the grandparents. Taking and making time to listen to, and to communicate with, God, our Creator, Redeemer and Sustainer, is foremost and centrally a beginning and a continuing practice, every day, necessary for a Jesus-following journey.

SIMPLICITY WITH A PURPOSE

For my grandparents, and many others of the Anabaptist persuasion, out of authentic piety – reverence for God and sincere respect for others – evolved the practice of simplicity. We live in an age of consumerism. We have often worshiped at the altar of materialism, with a mantra espousing, "They who die with the most toys win!" It is not, of course, that material things are bad. We need the material to live.

We are material. Jesus came as material, as expressed and celebrated in Incarnation. While material possessions are neither good or bad in and of themselves, it is the stewardship of material things that greatly matters. As someone has stated, "Do we love things and use people; or do we love people and use things?" Our coveting and hoarding of things evidence the problem. When we engage in materialism out of balance, we risk the danger of engaging in idolatry.

When hoarding, we not only bring harm to self, we also harm others. Simplicity lifestyle is associated with equity. Do we seek to live simply so that others may simply live? In Luke's Gospel (3:11) we read, "The person with two coats should share with those who have none, and the one who has food should do the same." I admired my paternal grandparents' consistent lifestyle, one of contentment, with basic comforts of life balanced with an intentional simplicity. I offer an example, which I have come to call, "The Contrast of Two Closets."

One season I lived with my grandparents for three weeks, while in residency working on a Doctor of Ministry degree in the Philadelphia, PA area. On a particular evening, while my grandpa and grandma were away from home, I was overcome with curiosity about walking into their bedroom and looking around. I gave into my curiosity and gave a look. What I found has left an indelible impression upon me. Their bedroom was relatively small, very clean and neat, and frugally, sparsely decorated. But what really amazed me was their clothing closet. There I found four or five outfits for both my grandparents. All garments were clean, neatly pressed, and hanging in a row. I was astonished at the simplicity of so few clothing items!

It was less than one month later, back home with my family in North Carolina, one night my wife, Karen, and I were awakened in a startling manner! A loud noise erupted from our master bedroom walk-in closet area. Upon investigating, we learned that the enormous weight of our many clothing garments had caused the clothing rod to collapse. Our clothes were lying on the closet floor in a huge heap.

I have not forgotten and have attempted to act by reducing my clothing inventory, the contrast of my grandparents' frugal and few garments contrasted with my over-abundant amount of clothing – too many, in fact, to ever wear them all. Do we practice a simplicity which derives from authentic piety which concerns itself with equity and fairness for all?

CHARITY – SEEKING GOD'S JUSTICE; SHOWING CHRIST'S MERCY

My final grandparent gleaning for life lessons is about their charity toward others. Here I am referring to charity as acts of love and grace. I would also describe this charity as seeking to share God's justice and to show Christ's mercy. Grandpa and grandma had a heart for the down and out and the hurting. For instance, I recall them frequently visiting a neighbor in their community whom many labeled as an outcast. He was dealing with a mental illness, during a day and time, and a culture, in which many dealing with a disease of this type would be criticized and ostracized. Gratefully, grandpa and grandma showed compassion and stayed in contact with this man and with his family.

I am thankful for the lineage and legacy passed on through my ancestors, including my Kurtz grandparents. They were fellow struggling sojourners, like all of us. Yet, amid the challenges and opportunities they encountered, they did the best they could with the resources they had. I give thanks for the many life lessons I learned from their lives, including the lessons of piety, simplicity and charity.

SCRIPTURE REFERENCES: Deuteronomy 2:4, 12:1; Matthew 6:33; Mark 9:50; Luke 9:25, 12:15; John 1:43; Acts 2:42; Romans 12:18; I Corinthians 7:29-31; Ephesians 5:15; I Thessalonians 4:11.

QUESTIONS FOR REFLECTION AND DISCUSSION:

1. Christianity is not about individualism. Rather, as Jesus followers, we are the body, the community of Christ. The body has many parts and each and all are integral and important to the whole. Read I Corinthians 12:12-31. According to this biblical passage, why is community necessary and valued?

2. In relationships, what are the potential problems with over-dependency? What are the possible difficulties with being fiercely independent? Rather than overly dependent or extremely independent, what might be a healthier relationship path?

3. How would you define a life of authentic piety?

4. In what ways might a lifestyle of intentional simplicity be a helpful antidote to the materialism of our culture?

5. What are the connections between authentic piety and genuine charity?

PRAYER: Dear Heavenly Father, thank you for the ancestors in our lives who have taught us in many ways. Like us, they are not perfect, yet even despite their limitations and imperfections we have discovered through their example life lessons helping us to navigate and celebrate the journey. Lord, help us glean and gain prudent principles and healthy habits from others which will help us further Your Kingdom on earth as it is in heaven. For Christ's sake. Amen.

CHAPTER TWENTY-ONE

DORI

Tender-Hearted, Tough-Skinned, and Spirit-Led

Be kind to one another, tenderhearted, forgiving
one another, as God in Christ forgave you.
-Ephesians 4:32

It was one of those relationship rough patches. As lead pastor, I had just been celebrating our church staff and members good cooperation and positive communication. We had come through a long stretch of excellent ministry momentum, accompanied by sweet harmony and strong growth. But now that wonderful harmony was seemingly dissipating as the days slowly and painfully grinded on with grudges and impasse.

I needed some consolation. My heart was heavy. I needed some consultation. My mind was confused. My thoughts turned to Dori. Dori was a long-time member of our congregation. She knew the history of our congregation. More importantly, she knew Jesus. By her fruit, by her persona, it was evidenced that she spent regular time in discussion with Divinity. I needed some of her God-given wisdom. I desired a portion of her Christ-centered compassion, along with a dose of her "Dori discernment."

I reached out to Dori. We met. We prayed. We shared. Dori patiently listened to my burdened heart. I poured out to her about the hateful words and behavior, and resulting hurt, that had been unleashed between parties in our church family. These were persons who claimed to follow Jesus Christ as Savior and Lord. Some of them were congregational leaders. Many looked to them for guidance and direction, as concerns living a life of Christian discipleship. Now, these persons in dueling dissension had become discouraging disappointments in the life of our faith community. What were we to do? What was I, as lead pastor, to do? How would this dissenting dilemma find resolution?

I was angry. I had been clinically trained to know that beneath anger there is deep hurt. Yet at the time I was living with reptilian response. How could these persons bring such damaging toxicity into our church family, just when the harmony and ministry momentum had been so good and right and strong? How could they do this? All these questions and emotions I verbally vomited toward Dori, who carefully and kindly practiced active listening.

Following a long while of listening, and a season of prayer, and some silent moments together, Dori spoke. "Michael, I hear and, as a member of this church family, I feel your pain. This is a concerning situation. It is deeply wrong, the way persons, who call themselves Jesus followers, are treating one another with such disrespect and disregard. Yet, I invite you, as our spiritual leader, to not overreact. We need your steadiness and emotional stability, especially for a time such as this. In this spirit of not overreacting, I share with you a saying my mom often shared with us children during our growing up days. Her words have stayed with me and have helped me many times in my leadership roles in the business world. When I faced conflictual circumstances and difficult relationships, mom would often say, "Dori, remember, when someone is difficult, you will be okay if you practice being tender-hearted and tough-skinned."

Decades have passed since this consultation with Dori, and still the terms, and more importantly the practices of being, tender-hearted and tough-skinned, continue to inform and guide my relationship responses. They help provide a proven path to staying connected to another, while establishing and maintaining healthy relationship boundaries when a relationship is stressed and strained. Tender-hearted practices call us to seek to practice empathy and try compassion toward another. Herein, one seeks to place themselves in another's shoes. This is not about excusing bad behavior, but it is about possibly explaining the negativity, hopefully leading to better understanding of the other.

On the other hand, tough-skinned practices guide us in demonstrating assertive sharing and enforcing healthy boundaries, especially when things are breaking down. A tough-skinned response includes not taking things personally. Seek to not be overly sensitive and reactive to unkind and possibly unjust treatment and talk. This approach often prevents the negative from escalating, providing more opportunity for lowering the emotional temperature and increasing the possibility of constructive conversation.

Upon further reflection of "Dori's Didactic," I have added a third principle for my own guidance in navigating difficult relationship dynamics. It is Spirit-led. Tender-hearted. Tough-skinned. And Spirit-led. It is my conviction that I need divine discernment when it comes to decision-making. I do not possess wisdom on my own. Therefore, before I engage in tender-hearted or tough-skinned choices and behaviors, I need God's guidance. Spirit-led reminds, and calls, me to a time of meditation and reflection with the Holy Spirit, prior to taking any form of action. I conclude this chapter with a few considerations of, and reflections upon, the practices of being: Tender-hearted; Tough-skinned; and Spirit-led.

TENDER-HEARTED

In our interpersonal relationships we all need to give and to receive love and compassion. As we consider the term tender-hearted, we might consider the root word, tend. To tend to someone, or something, is to give adequate attention. To tend to another means to look after a person, providing them with necessary attention and support. When we add "er" to the verb "tend," we discover an adjective, or a descriptive term. In our Christian terminology we are familiar with the encouraging and inspiring term, Jesus, our tender Shepherd. Of course, good shepherds tend to their sheep. They care for them by looking after their needs. Thus, they are "tend-ers" of those who are recipients of their care.

Jesus, our good and tender Shepherd, watches over us with tender care. Tender care indicates extra attention or considerate care is provided, making another feel very special and loved. To be tender with another person is to be very kind and gentle. A tender look or a tender touch can be ways of showing tender-hearted care. Tender-hearted behavior toward another, then, emanates from perceiving the value of the other. It is generated out of respect and compassion for another person with whom we are in relationship. We all need and crave the receiving of tender-hearted care. And we all need to share tender-hearted care. Ephesians reminds us, "Be kind and tenderhearted to one another, forgiving each other just as in Christ God forgave you" (Ephesians 4:32).

TOUGH-SKINNED

Tough-skinned, as employed here, speaks of several meanings. We are using the term here as: not being easily offended so that one may make some difficult and differentiated decisions for another who may not, for example, be setting and observing healthy, functional relationship boundaries. To be tender-hearted is a necessary and positive practice (as noted and affirmed in the above paragraphs). However, when the tender-hearted care is abused and taken advantage of, tough love (including tough-skinned response) is called for. This tough love is especially to be demonstrated by the leader, the shepherd, of a flock, who is responsible for helping to establish and maintain a safe and functional environment for the members of the shared community. Tough-skinned practices, including the practice of tough love, is necessary whenever members of the family or community go rogue.

We need to remind ourselves that the motive behind tough love, with a tough-skinned approach, is always, when rightly motivated and correctly done, generated out of the goal of restoration. We wish to restore relationships for Kingdom's sake. Jesus provides tough-skinned, tough-love guidance in Matthew 18:15-20. "If a person refuses to listen to fellow believers, tell it to the church; and if he refuses to listen even to the church, treat him as you would a pagan or a tax collector." (Matthew 18:17). These are hard choices and difficult decisions, not to be taken lightly, and employed sparingly. Tough-skinned choices are usually last resort actions. Nonetheless, tough skinned and tough love is mandatory at times to establish proper accountability, healthy systems and prayerfully reconciled relationships.

SPIRIT LED

As important and as necessary as both practices of tender-hearted and tough-skinned are for establishing and maintaining healthy and functional relationships, there is a third practice which I submit is the guiding litmus test for employing any relationship behavioral strategy. It is the practice of being Spirit-led. A Spirit-led posture and practice acknowledges humankind does not possess the total and final picture concerning any relationship. We need Holy Spirit guidance and intervention in our decision-making process. We require and request divine discernment regarding all our relationship diagnoses and prescriptions in life. This mindset and approach, then, recognizes and readily admits our own short sightedness and shortcomings. We arrive at tough choices with humility rather than arrogance. We may be incorrect in our assessment and judgments. We must be open to, and allow for, correction and amendment of our advice to and admonitions of others. Our leadership concerning relationship choices and advisements must, when properly administered, be done within the context of community. The leader needs to make recommendations and take relationship actions only within the parameters of community accountability, never solo.

This community context seems to be one of the primary points that Jesus makes in Matthew, chapter 18, on retribution and restoration of relationships within the faith community. "If he refuses to listen, tell it to the church" (Matthew 18:17a). Within the community of faith, the Holy Spirit often gives guidance and discernment through the checks and balances, as well as a plurality of perspectives provided through the gathered saints.

I am indelibly thankful to God for the presence and discernment of Dori at a critical juncture in my pastoring of a congregation, and in helping to shape relationship decision-making in my life. The three relationship legs of being tender-hearted, tough-skinned and Spirit-led seem wise ways to keep a relationship strong and balanced.

SCRIPTURE REFERENCES: Tender-hearted – Galatians 5:22-23; Ephesians 4:32; Colossians 3:12; I Peter 3:8-10. Tough-skinned – 2 Samuel 12:1-14; Proverbs 13:24; Matthew 18:15-20, 21:13; Galatians 6:1-5; Hebrews 10:24-25. Spirit-led – Psalm 143:10; Matthew 4:1; John 14:26; Romans 8:9,14; Galatians 5:18; Ephesians 4:30.

QUESTIONS FOR REFLECTION AND DISCUSSION:
1. What are some characteristics of a tender-hearted approach to another person?
2. How would you describe tough-skinned? How might tender-hearted and tough-skinned approaches provide a needed balance in a relationship?

3. Read and reflect upon Matthew 18:15-20. In what ways do you see Jesus' instructions in Matthew 18 include a call to compassion and a call to accountability?

4. What does it mean to be a Spirit-led person? How might a Spirit-led approach to relationship guidance make a positive difference?

PRAYER: Spirit of the Living God, fall afresh on us. We need you, O God! We need your discernment, your wisdom and your guidance all the days of our life. In our own relationships, and in attempting to encourage and assist other relationships, give us your discernment so that we may know when to practice tender-hearted compassion and when to provide tough-skinned, tough love, for the sake of healthy interpersonal dynamics and ultimately reconciliation of relationships. May all these decisions and interactions be Spirit-led, so that we have the perspective and power of your Holy Spirit, all given and guided through Christ's community of faith. For the cause of your Kingdom, O Lord we pray. Amen

A FRIEND IS SOMEONE
WHO KNOWS ALL ABOUT
YOU AND STILL LOVES YOU.
-Elbert Hubbard

(Authenticity coupled with
unconditional love and acceptance).

CHAPTER TWENTY-TWO

SAM AND LINDA

A Place and a People of Sanctuary (A Safe Place)

My Place of Refuge and Safety – Psalm 91:2

As a young adult bachelor, I recall many days of questioning and wondering what my relationship future would look like? I did not surmise that I was called to a life of singleness. Yet, I was going through a dry and lonely spell. Courting was next to slim and none. Prospects did not seem promising. As some of us undergraduates at the college I attended had joked, at least we thought of it as a joke: "We will be a member of the 'bachelor-to-the-rapture' fraternity!"

At this point and time in my life I was in my mid-20s, and I was a high school teacher and coach. I certainly enjoyed this vocation and looked forward to the future. Yet, the thought of a future alone was not part of my present pondering and plan. While teaching I learned to know and grew to love a couple of co-teachers, Sam and Linda. Sam and Linda were a married couple who opened their home and their hearts to me, and to many others. Their door was always open. They regularly seemed to have patient and actively listening hearts. Their Christ-like hospitality and gracious acceptance provided me with a lot of help and much hope as I sojourned the single seek-and-search phase of my life.

I felt so welcomed and affirmed whenever I entered the home of Sam and Linda. Looking back, I probably should have left a cash payment on their coffee table for each visit. It was therapy. It was healing time. It was hospitality on a stick! In their presence I experienced safety, acceptance and belonging. Sam offered a steady, calm and supportive persona. Linda radiated an enthusiastic encouragement which, I reasoned, could bring a dead man back to life!

Speaking of a dead man resurrected, I am reminded of Jesus at Bethany. Bethany, several miles outside of the holy city of Jerusalem, is the place to which Jesus often retreated. It seemed like a place of sanctuary for him. More specifically, he would find and enjoy the much-needed hospitality, at the home of his dear friends Martha, Mary and Lazarus. It was one place where Jesus could let down his hair and relax. Here he found acceptance. Here he was like part of the family. Here he could find R & R. A visit with these folks renewed Jesus for the journey ahead. A bed and breakfast and a place for just being, brought vigor back to his bones! The Bethany family practiced such welcoming hospitality. As scripture puts it, "As Jesus travelled, he came to a village (Bethany) where a woman named Martha opened her home to him" (Luke 10:38).

Wow! Can you imagine? Opening your home to Jesus, and he stops by to stay a spell! And the reality is we do have the choice to invite Jesus to come and live with us, or not! If we invite Jesus, he will come and live in, and with, us forever! In Revelation 3:20 are these words of eternal hospitality, "Here I am! I stand at the door and knock. If anyone hears my voice and opens the door, I will come in and eat with them and they with me." The wonderful, grace-filled hospitality of entering a common space, fellowshipping and breaking bread together around table. This is the stuff of safety, acceptance and belonging!

"Come on in!" "Sit a spell!" "How are you doing?" "What's on your mind and heart today?" These and other welcoming statements were frequently received from my friends Sam and Linda. Fortunate indeed are those folks who find a friend who "loveth at all times." What a treasured gift are those in our life who offer us Christ-like hospitality, evidenced through their place of safety, their persona and hearts of acceptance and their non-judgmental posture. I affirm everyone needs a place like Bethany and I assert everybody needs friends like Sam and Linda in their lives.

SCRIPTURE REFERENCES: 2 Samuel 17:27-29; Luke 10:30-37; Acts 16:34; Hebrews 13:2; Revelation 3:20; Luke 10:38; John 3:16, 11:5; Psalm 100:3; Luke 18:16; Ephesians 2:17-22; Psalm 27:5, 91:1-2; Proverbs 18:10; Isaiah 4:6.

QUESTIONS FOR REFLECTION AND DISCUSSION:

1. Recall a place, a space, a people where you have experienced an "at home" feeling. What characteristics create this sense of belonging for you? How might you enable another to encounter that same place of Christlike hospitality?

2. Read the story of The Good Samaritan, Luke 10:30-37. What is taught about Christlike hospitality in this passage?

3. Poet Robert Frost wrote, "Home is the place that when you go there, they have to take you in." I take it that this Frost quote speaks to the subject of belonging. We belong to family. We belong at home. We hope and pray for this reality for everyone, however, sadly some do not have this

experience. What are some ways in which we may help ensure that others, especially the vulnerable, have a place of acceptance and belonging.

4. Reflect upon Revelation 3:20. Jesus wishes to live with us and to live within us. These words of scripture assure us that if we open the door to Christ, he will constantly fellowship, and continually feast, with us.

PRAYER: O Lord, thank you for seeking us, finding us, and living in and through us! You promise your permanent presence in and with us if we believe and receive you. Your word tells us, "If we open the door of our heart to you, you will come in and dine with us." Or, again, your word assures, "If you abide in me, I will abide in you." Heavenly Parent, your presence provides us security, your grace grants us acceptance, and your hospitality never leaves us alone or deserted. We experience authentic and permanent peace, for we belong to you. Amen.

FUNCTIONAL RELATIONSHIP IS NEITHER OVERLY DEPENDENT OR FIERCELY INDEPENDENT BUT, RATHER INTERDEPENDENT.

-Michael Kurtz

(Avoid over functioning or under functioning in a relationship).

CHAPTER TWENTY-THREE

REGGIE

A Good Sense of Humor

"A Merry Heart Does Good" - Proverbs 17:22

I count myself blessed to have grown up in a supportive neighborhood with great neighbors. One of those great neighbors was Reggie. From my perspective, what made Reggie a great neighbor, and a great person, was his positive posture toward life. He possessed a wonderful sense of humor coupled with the fact that he did not take himself too seriously. What made this upbeat attitude even more amazing is that if anyone had a reason to be down and out, it would have been Reggie.

A military veteran, Reggie, had been severely wounded in the Korean Conflict. Shrapnel found his body and he was rendered paraplegic for life. I'm certain Reggie had some down, discouraging days. However, those of us who spent significant time with him very rarely saw a sad side of him.

Reggie possessed one of the best senses of humor I've ever witnessed. His frequent laughter was contagious. Just a little time spent with him was like a balm for the spirit. Reminds me of the scripture which states, "A cheerful heart is good medicine" (Proverbs 17:22a). Or, again, "A happy heart makes the face cheerful" (Proverbs 15:13a). That's it! Being around Reggie was like a helpful dose of medicine for a sad, sickened spirit. Somehow, he willed himself to merriment while wheeling around in a wheelchair.

He did not permit his so-called handicap to hinder his healthy humor! While Reggie could have wallowed in his self-pity, instead he chose not to take himself too seriously. There was much in life to be thankful for. And he found it. There was much to be positive about. And he chose that path – The path and perspective which chooses to see the glass half full instead of half empty. Reggie inspired me and many others with his engagement in, and zest for, life, despite very challenging circumstances. His decision and his resolve were to not live "under the circumstances," but rather to realistically accept his situation and then through his faith, fortitude, family and friends to creatively adapt doing the very best that he could do.

This positive outlook, coupled with his interest in others and their life, precluded him from throwing pity parties. Instead of being consumed with himself and dominated by what some would label liabilities and disabilities, Reggie demonstrated an interest in others through asking questions and showing genuine concern. These are some of the qualities that made Reggie a good neighbor and a good friend.

SCRIPTURE REFERENCES: Psalm 144:15; Proverbs 15:13; Ecclesiastes 3:12, 9:7. Leviticus 19:18; Proverbs 14:21; Matthew 22:39; Mark 12:31; Romans 13:10, 15:2. Exodus 14:1-4; I Peter 5:6-7; Revelation 14:6-7.

QUESTIONS FOR REFLECTION AND DISCUSSION:

1. The study of psychosomatics informs us that our attitude can influence our physical health. In what ways may "a merry heart" be medicine to our minds and bodies?
2. Circumstances in life can seemingly make or break us. When we face some difficult times, how may we keep from living "under the circumstances"?
3. My friend, Reggie, was a paraplegic who chose the path of positive perseverance instead of participating in pity parties. What are some healthy and helpful practices that may preclude us from going critical and negative?
4. It has been said, "Take yourself less seriously. And take God more seriously." Do you agree that this philosophy for life is essential? Why or why not?

PRAYER: God of Joy, we praise you for the gifts of good humor and laughter! For those who demonstrate and share levity and laughter among us, we give thanks. We affirm, a merry and happy heart is like a soothing medicine for our spirits. Please help us to not take ourselves too seriously and to take you, O God, more seriously, and in doing so finding a joy and serenity that adds quality and goodness to our days and to others. For the cause of Christ, we pray. Amen.

CHAPTER TWENTY-FOUR

Hagey

A Surrogate Grandparent

Stand up in the presence of the aged, show respect for
the elderly and revere your God. -Leviticus 19:32

I suppose I was around the age of ten when I first began visiting our next-door neighbor, Hagey. At the time Hagey was in his mid-70s, his wife of fifty plus years had recently died, and he was a lonely man dealing with deep grief and loss. I'm not certain what help a ten-year-old boy could offer to a grieving soul. Anyway, Hagey and I hit it off from the very beginning. He seemed to like my company, and I liked his kindness. I also liked the pecan sandies he kept in his kitchen cookie jar. Plus, I liked watching the Western shootout cowboy movies he frequently watched on his television, which I was not permitted to view at home.

Hagey had a Chihuahua named Ginger. At first Ginger wasn't sure about me coming into their home and her yapping seemed to never cease. But as my visits were more frequent, she began to bark less and less. In fact, after several months, Ginger began to warm up to me, and eventually would sit on my lap during our visits.

MINISTRY IN MUTUAL GRIEF

I surmise, looking back, that Hagey and I enjoyed one another's company and perhaps could join a bit in our respective grief, as I had recently lost a dog that I had owned for many years. A seventy-five-year-old widower, a ten-year-old boy and a five-year-old Chihuahua made quite a trio. I did not realize back then, but I truly believe that our lives ministered to one another amid loneliness and grief. I found, and gave, help and hope amid conversation, cookies and a Chihuahua. I suppose we were living out Galatians 6:2 without even being aware of doing so, "Carry each other's burdens, and in this way, you will fulfill the law of Christ."

Hagey had been in the coal mining industry in West Virginia for many years prior to moving to our North Carolina neighborhood. He had relatives in our area, including a son, so after retiring he made the move to Ashe County. To occupy his time, and to fulfill one of his interests, he purchased a cattle farm about two miles from his residence. Many times, after school I would ride with him to the farm to feed the cattle, Ginger riding along in the front seat of his Pontiac.

INTERGENERATIONAL RELATIONSHIPS

I had many visits and many trips to the cattle farm with Hagey over the years. He had become a dear friend to me. I also think he became a surrogate grandparent to me. He seemed to fill a void for me in the grandfathering category. Both sets of my grandparents lived five hundred miles away from me, in Pennsylvania. On average I would see my grandparents a couple times a year. In Hagey, whom I visited weekly, I discovered a next-door grandfather figure.

THE LOSS OF A FRIEND

I enjoyed some wonderful years with my neighbor and friend, Hagey. But when I was sixteen, he passed away. I will never forget the day. After school I noticed there were several cars at Hagey's house. That was unusual. I went to the front door. His son greeted me and asked me to come in and to have a seat. He then broke the sad news to me, that his dad, Hagey, had died.

This was my first experience of losing to death someone considered close. It hit me hard. Ginger was there and you could tell she was disconcerted and confused. I asked Hagey's son if Ginger and I could sit on the basement steps for a while. We did. I remember grieving with Ginger, tears streaming down my face as she looked up at me with those big, brown Chihuahua eyes. I stroked her silky coat, shiny because, I recall Hagey said, he fed her eggs mixed in her dogfood because that would make a dog's coat shine. After that time with Ginger on the steps, I excused myself and headed home.

Hagey was gone. I grieved his loss for a long time. But I am grateful to God for placing him in my life, at a time in which I think I helped him, and I know he helped me. Who would have thought that a seventy-five-year-old man, a ten-year- old boy, and a five-year-old Chihuahua would have developed a close relationship? You never know, sometimes the least likely become fast friends.

SCRIPTURE REFERENCES: Psalm 23; Proverbs 17:17, 18:2, 18:13, 27:7; John 8:32, 15:12-15; Galatians 6:2; James 1:19.

QUESTIONS FOR REFLECTION AND DISCUSSION:
1. A mid-70s retired man and a 10-year-old schoolboy become friends. How might intergenerational relationships be a blessing, and what may people of different generations learn from one another?
2. Loneliness is considered an epidemic in our culture and era. How can we address and help resolve loneliness both in our own life and in the lives of others?
3. Look at Galatians 6:2. In what ways does "bearing each other's burdens," constitute, "fulfilling the law of Christ"?
4. Grief is difficult and painful to endure. Yet, upon reflection, grief is a gift from God, provided we receive the gift by working through stages of grief with honesty and perseverance. What are some of the stages of grief and how might each one help provide healing?

PRAYER: Healer of our souls, we pray for the lonely - the least, the last and the lost. For those who find themselves shut in and shut out. We pray they may find friendship and belonging in this sometimes unfriendly and isolating world. May we be a part of the solution, fighting the loneliness epidemic in our day and time in our own corner of the world. Empower us with courage and compassion to reach out in personal ways to someone in our community who finds themselves lonely. May we be especially attentive to those lonely and in the valley of grief following the loss of a loved one. We pray this in the name of the One who walks with us through our loss and grief, providing us with grace, strength and peace, even Christ our Lord. Amen.

Hagey's Home

CHAPTER TWENTY-FIVE

BETTY JO

A Willing Spirit, A Servant's Heart, An Open Mind

To Serve is to Love

Betty Jo was the kind of Jesus follower and church member every pastor is blessed to have in the faith family. Through the years of serving as her pastor I saw her willing spirit and servant's heart evidenced over and over. She was willing to step up when there was a need. And she was willing to step out, serving others with God's justice and Christ's mercy.

OPEN-HANDED LIVING

In Betty Jo's genuine humility approach to life there was an absence of presumption and an entitlement mindset. That is, she displayed a disciple disposition, with open hands, to both receive and to give as the Lord provides, rather than grasping and clinging through life with clenched fists. Blessed are those with an open hand posture toward life, for they shall receive. Betty Jo was an example of, and an inspiration for, open-handed living. Isn't it instructive that we arrive in life with our hands clenched tightly, while we leave this earth with our hands wide open?! O that we might learn the secret of open-handed living, for God cannot place his gifts into, nor share through, hands selfishly, tightly clasped.

Through open hands and a servant's heart I watched Betty Jo love and care for others. When we needed cookies for fellowship time, she came through. When we were looking for a children's Sunday school teacher, she stepped up. Our mid-week intergenerational ministry was seeking a table parent for the evening meal, and she served as a nurturing table parent to several young children. Then, when our congregation was looking to bring on staff a Christian Educator, Betty Jo's name surfaced, and she was eventually hired. Again, with a humble servant's heart, she did not seek this staff position. Yet, when she called, she prayed, she discerned, and she accepted the ministry role on our church staff. To serve with Betty Jo was one of the great ministry joys of my life. Her willingness to serve and her humility in serving were instructive and inspiring to all of us within her serving sphere. In the words of Matthew 23 (verses 11,12), "The greatest among you will be your servant. For whoever exalts themselves will be humbled, and whoever humbles themselves will be exalted."

WIDEN THE CIRCLE

In addition to Betty Jo's willing spirit and servant's heart, she possessed an open mind. She sought to show God's acceptance and love to all. Each person is created in the image of God; therefore, each person is of infinite value and worth. The DNA of Divinity is present, even when suppressed and unexpressed, in every human being. Often, the presence and grace message of Christ is evidenced and expressed in the least likely. Betty Jo cared deeply about, and advocated for, the down and out, the disenfranchised. Often, she volunteered at the downtown crisis assistance center relating to and reaching out to many who would be counted by many as the least and the last of society.

Betty Jo stepped up to help through her willing and giving spirit. She touched lives for Jesus through her servant's heart. And she sought to widen the circle, including the shut in and the shut out, through an open mind.

SCRIPTURE REFERENCES: Joshua 22:5; Psalm 51:12, 119:111-113; Matthew 5:41; Mark 14:32-42; Matthew 23:11,12; Mark 10:43-45; 2 Corinthians 4:5; Galatians 5:13; Proverbs 1:19,20; Matthew 13:9; Acts 17:22-23; Romans 12:18; I Corinthians 9:20-22; James 1:19.

QUESTIONS FOR REFLECTION AND DISCUSSION:

1. Betty Jo, I affirm, displayed a disciple (of Jesus) disposition. How would you describe a disciple disposition?
2. Look at your hands. First, study them with palms wide open and turned upward. Next, clench your hands into fists. Describe the differences, and what these hand postures possibly say about life.
3. Why is humility so centrally connected to a servant's heart? Read Mark 10:42-45. What does this passage say about Jesus following and humility?
4. Someone has shared, "A closed mind is like a closed parachute!" Reflect upon St. Paul's experience of open-mindedness and diplomacy in ancient Athens in Acts 17:22,23.

PRAYER: All-knowing and All-loving God, we praise you for calling us to be your people. Through your son's example and empowerment, we are to develop and display a servant's heart. Jesus, who was God, emptied and humbled himself even to death on the cross that we sinners may be saved. O Lord, may we help, and not hinder, your Kingdom. May we draw the circle wider, and in doing so may we point more souls to the Bread of Life – one beggar showing another beggar to the bread. In the name of Christ our Lord. Amen.

CHAPTER TWENTY-SIX

KEITH

A Team Player

Sticks in a bundle are unbreakable. -Kenyan Proverb

Keith was a part of our church ministry team. He was Director of Music at our congregation. Sometimes, sadly, Directors of Music and Pastors can be infamous for not having the best relationships. Perhaps they become territorial in terms of music in worship, if you can imagine! Maybe it's their eccentric personalities and tenuous temperaments, both music staff and pastoral staff can be interesting to say the least. Chemistry is not always positive. Tensions can arise. "Staff" infection can present. At times, the temple Levites and temperamental priests have their peculiar ways and don't practice harmony. Lord, in your mercy, hear our prayer, and forgive us!

CHEMISTRY GOOD

Thankfully, the Levites and the Priests can get it right! Keith was a joy to work with. Doing ministry and leading worship with him was a delight. The chemistry felt right. There was mutual appreciation. Planning of worship happened with cooperation and complementation. Leading worship was shared without competition. The outcome resulted in a praise and worship of God that seemed to be led in unity and with integrity. There was an admission that God was working in and through us despite ourselves and our shortcomings. We were broken, and we were broken together before Holy God, Righteous Lord, as we sought to point to Jesus in the gathered worship of the faith community.

I appreciated very much the genuine humility coupled with the great talent that Keith possessed and brought to the planning and the leading of worship. He was a wonderful composer and had written much music, which he sometimes shared with our church family in worship. He was also a contemplative soul. It was evidenced that he spent intentional devotional time with God. For one, it showed in his music. Sometimes, as he played the music prelude at the beginning of our worship services, I would get lost in wonder and praise as he brought the keyboard to such an inspired life! Then, I would soon return to reality and remind myself that I too was co-leading this worship service, so I needed to focus upon my responsibilities of presiding. But God used Keith to enable me to worship at the same time as I was responsible for leading worship. That, I found over the years of leading worship, for hundreds of Sunday mornings, was a rarity, and a gift. Yet Keith had a gift and presentation that fostered focused worship.

I count myself blessed to have worked and worshiped with Keith for nearly a decade. He brought so much to the table. He was so talented. He walked closely with God. He had ministry and worship related insights and ideas that greatly enriched our worship experiences and services. And he did so unassumingly.

A CONFIDANTE

Even though Keith was super talented; Even though he could compose beautifully captivating music; and even though his keyboard playing was so wonderfully inspiring, as someone put it, "If that doesn't light your fire, your wood is wet!"; Even though all those attributes, talents, and a humble attitude to boot, I think having Keith as a confidante was the most treasured. We engaged in many conversations over the years. He was a soul I could trust. Leaders cannot safely share with everyone. They must be prudent and careful in whom they confide. Keith and I found trust and confidence in one another. We connected. We related. And we trusted one another. I knew that what I shared with Keith would be kept in total confidence, and he knew the same was offered to him by me.

I am grateful for the times of fellowship, friendship and worship with Keith. Co-leading gathered worship of God's people was both a holy privilege and a joyful blessing. The Levite and the Priest discovered heaven-sent harmony serving together.

SCRIPTURE REFERENCES: Psalm 33:3, 34:1-3; 84:4-5,10; 104:33-34. Psalm 133:1-3; Romans 12:5-6; I Corinthians 1:10. Psalm 133:1; Psalm 133:1; Proverbs 18:24, 27:9; I Thessalonians 5:11.

QUESTIONS FOR REFLECTION AND DISCUSSION:
1. Read Psalm 34:1-3. It has been stated that in heaven we will worship God forever, and here on earth our worship experiences are rehearsal for what we will do for all eternity. How important is corporate, gathered worship to you? Why?
2. Have you encountered lack of harmony in gathered worship? How do you know when this occurs? What does it feel like? What is the solution?
3. What are some practices and personal characteristics which contribute to team harmony and unity?

4. To whom may you confide in confidence and with trust? Are you a trusted confidante to another?

PRAYER: God of Peace and Harmony, forgive us for our false pride and foolish divisions. We are placed on this earth to love and worship you, and to love one another through your amazing grace. How it must break your heart when we quibble, argue and fight, without actively listening to one another. We desire mercy for ourselves while wanting justice for others. Help us to humble ourselves so that together we may worship you in unity and peace.

Thank you for the people in our lives with whom we may share in confidence, providing us with the assurance that they will not break trust. Those who help in keeping, instead of harming, harmony in the community of faith. Lord, may we also be trustworthy and dependable in our relationships with others. For the sake of harmony and unity in the Body of Christ we pray. Amen.

AFTERWORD

There is nothing on this earth more to be prized than true friendship.
-Thomas Aquinas

My hope and prayer is that this work on friendship will encourage us to remember, reflect upon, and perhaps renew our appreciation for the instructing and inspiring persons God has placed in our lives along the journey. Proverbs 27:17 states, "As iron sharpens iron, so friends sharpen one another."

We were not created to do this thing called life all alone. We require the support, encouragement and accountability that authentic friendship provides. The phrase, "Iron sharpens iron," suggests that through our relationships we can sharpen each other by lending mutual support, feedback and challenges. True friendship includes tender love and tough love. Authentic friendship subscribes to the much-needed yet rarely practiced proverbial phrase, "Tell the truth in love."

Two pieces of iron can sharpen each other through the process of being rubbed together. So too, as people interrelate, confronting and comforting one another, they are enabled to change and grow and get better. Every relationship in our life offers opportunities and challenges for learning and growing.

Let us thank God for the people placed in our path. May we possess a posture toward life which includes open minds and hearts toward others. Most of all, let us be grateful for the faithful friends in our life who have helped to shape and form our faith. Many have led us closer to Jesus, whether by bustin' through roofs, lending listening ears, or sharing tender and tough love. No matter our interactions, may our relationship efforts bless and strengthen us, that we may assist in building God's Kingdom on earth as in heaven. O Lord, we thank you for the ordinary people in our lives who have exhibited extraordinary faith!

-Michael Kurtz, 2024

ABOUT THE AUTHOR

Michael Kurtz is a pastor, therapist and author, living in the majestic mountains of northwestern North Carolina. Following several years of teaching high school English and coaching athletic teams, Michael attended and graduated from Duke Divinity School. Following graduation, Pastor Kurtz served as lead pastor of seven United Methodist congregations over a forty-year-plus span.

Rev. Kurtz is married to Karen Christy Kurtz. Their immediate family includes, a son Joshua, his wife, Tara, and grandsons Wesley and Micah, a daughter Anna, and her husband, Adam. Kurtz enjoys time with family, hiking, playing guitar, singing, writing and golfing.

Michael's formal education includes: 1975, Lees-McRae, AA; 1977, Eastern Mennonite University, BA; 1984 Duke Divinity School, M Div; 1994, Palmer University, D Min. 1996, Licensed as Marriage and Family Therapist (NC #609).

Printed in the United States
by Baker & Taylor Publisher Services